Across the Spectrum

Across the Spectrum

What Color Are You?

Stephen Elkins-Jarrett

BUSINESS EXPERT PRESS

Across the Spectrum: What Color Are You?

First published in 2017 by
Business Expert Press, LLC
222 East 46th Street, New York, NY 10017
www.businessexpertpress.com

ISBN-13: 978-1-63157-705-5 (paperback)
ISBN-13: 978-1-63157-706-2 (e-book)

Business Expert Press Human Resource Management and Organizational Behavior Collection

Collection ISSN: 1946-5637 (print)
Collection ISSN: 1946-5645 (electronic)

Cover and interior design by Exeter Premedia Services Private Ltd., Chennai, India

First edition: 2017

10 9 8 7 6 5 4 3 2 1

Printed in the United States of America.

This book is dedicated to Mike Smith of Manskill Associates, who sadly died on June 28, 2009, and who taught me everything I know and set me on the right road, changing my career and lighting the touch paper on behavior by telling me:

> Stephen, you can achieve anything you want! The only thing stopping you is your lack of imagination and will power.

This man was a genius, my Guru, my mentor, and my life coach—I will never be able to repay him or thank him enough for a life-changing experience working with him! Thanks to Carly, Emily, and William—the loves of my life.

Thanks to Nick Skinner of Poppyfish People Development who helped me with all the graphics and his ability to use blue behaviors when I could not, and also thanks to Julie Sutton and Steve Berry for all their help and support in the past.

Abstract

Man has studied behavior for thousands of years: the ancient Greeks compared human behavior to earth, water, fire, and air; Freud, Jung, Fromm, Rodgers, and Pavlov have been fascinated by behavior. Psychologists have labeled behavioral types with words. Some of these models are lost to time like, Mar's facial shapes or Pavlov's canine types. Others, as old as the 1930s (Eric Fromm on which this book is based) are still used today. Myers-Briggs MBTI, Disc, and LIFO are still very popular in the western world as management tools. The problem with many of these models is you need to be "qualified" to use them, which is costly to administer. SPECTRUM is based on colors not words and is cheaper, easier, and understandable by all staff at all levels from day one. You thought it was complicated and confusing, maybe needed a degree in psychology to understand it? What is different about Spectrum? Well it does not categorize you into introvert or extrovert but rather on a continuum or spectrum between the two extremes. It also blends four primary colors into 18 styles—no one else does this. Think of red, what does that color say to you? Understand yourself and then learn how to tune into others, and for the first time understand that:—"We are taught as children to treat others the way that we would like to be treated, this is wrong! We have to start treating others as THEY would like to be treated!"

Keywords

behavior, body-language, change, facial expressions, leadership, management and culture, personality, profiling, psychology, psychometrics, self-help, style, voice

Contents

Preface

"We are taught as children to treat others how **WE** want to be treated, but this is wrong! We must start treating others how **THEY** would like to be treated!" But how can we do this if we are not them? Spectrum will quickly identify your preferred work style and another person's work style and then show you how to be more influential; keep control of situations and relationships; and be more powerful, persuasive, inspirational, and successful.

S	P	E	C	T	R	U	M
P	E	F	O	H	E	N	Y
E	R	F	M	R	A	D	S
C	S	E	M	O	L	E	E
I	O	C	U	U	L	R	L
F	N	T	N	G	Y	S	F
I	A	I	I	H		T	
C	L	V	C			A	
		E	A			N	
			T			D	
			I			I	
			O			N	
			N			G	

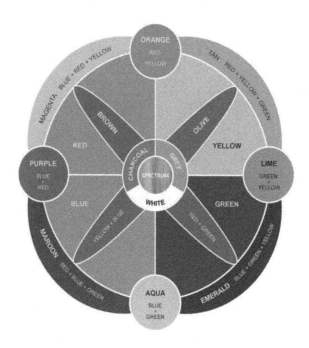

SPECIFIC
PERSONAL
EFFECTIVE
COMMUNICATION
THOROUGH
REALLY
UNDERSTANDING
MYSELF

By Stephen Elkins-Jarrett

CHAPTER 1

Introduction

I am the sole author of the dictionary that defines me!
—Zadie Smith, author from the book NW

What is this book all about? It is quite simply a book about behavior and making behavior simple to understand and help you become more influential.

It is not a book about personality nor is it a scientific or medical book, and it is not really about psychology, but it is simply a book about understanding your style.

If you went on a holiday to a foreign country, I would like to think that you would try to speak to the locals in their language and not just slower and louder in your own tongue. So why do we try to communicate to others in our style, and not in theirs?

Derren Brown said in his recent show,

There are only two things you can totally control, your thoughts and your actions.
—Miracles stage show London—2015

So here is a way to totally control your behaviors (actions) and thoughts (feelings).

For all my early life, it frustrated me that I never understood behavior, as my parents used to say to me, "Behave yourself—or else!" but I never knew what this meant. I think my parents were saying, do as you are told or else! Don't embarrass me, don't be too loud or talkative, sit still and shut up, go to bed when we tell you, and so on—it was all about controlling the children—not teaching us or understanding what behavior is. The funny or ironic thing is that our parents were telling us off for behaving like them. I was copying them.

Personality is the deep you, hidden from others, but behavior is on the surface that we can hear and see, and so the next time you hear someone say "it is a clash of personalities," tell them they are wrong. It is nearly always a clash of behaviors. For it to be a clash of personality you need to be them, or be their lifelong partner, sleep with them, and know their values and beliefs then you can have a clash of personality. A clash of behavior is what we get at work when we disagree or argue with another person when using an inappropriate style for the situation we are in—a Hawaiian shirt to a funeral.

How did I get here? How come I claim to know so much about one of the great mysteries of the last 4,000 years?

I started my career as a chef, where bad behavior and angry-head chefs were commonplace, and being aggressive seemed to me to be the norm. Then I left that career and went into the construction industry, again being aggressive or angry was the norm. If you didn't do as you were told you got hit or at least shouted at. At the same time, I was heavily involved in amateur dramatics and after some years of performing, directing, working backstage, and putting on four productions a year, I found myself playing Willie Mossop in the play Hobson's Choice by Harold Brighouse, a story of a downtrodden cobbler and an aggressive shoe shop owner and how their roles switch and Mossop ends up having the power and Hobson shrinks away—and this play, I believe, is where the expression "Hobson's Choice" came from, leaving Hobson with only one choice to let Mossop marry his daughter and take over the shop. The director of this play was Mike (Michael) Smith and he got us to role-play the characters, in periods before the play starts and even after the play finishes, so we could begin to understand the characters and empathize. Not everyone's cup of tea but I loved it and we got on well. When the show finished, he asked me what I did for a living and so I told him painting, decorating, and special effect paint finishing! He basically asked me, then and there, if I fancied being a "management consultant." I had no idea what one was or what they did and even if I had the right qualifications, but I did it. Richard Branson said, "If you ever get asked to do a job and think I am not sure if I can do that, do it and learn how to do it as you go. It is all I have ever done!"

So, I joined him in his consultancy, worked with him, watched him, observed him, and started my studies at night school, through distance learning, modular programs through universities, and colleges in the United Kingdom, which took me five years. I have continued to learn and develop, recently qualifying as a Cognitive Behavioral Therapist (CBT) counsellor, a Neuro linguistic programming (NLP) practitioner, and a life coach. And after five years, I was on my own. I was consulting businesses on strategy, delivering leadership training, and completing one-to-one coaching and large group facilitation for top businesses. I was working with refuse collectors to chief executive officers (CEOs), doctors, scientists, psychiatrists, solicitors and lawyers, and in every sector from construction to catering across the world. It proves that it is less about what you know and more about who you know and who is prepared to help you. Mike did just that. So, the next time someone needs help—give it to them—whatever it might be, give someone else the chance to develop. I have tried to do the same with my work colleagues over the years and feel that I have had some successes.

There are people wedded to other psychometrics and behavioral assessment tools and they find it hard to accept another model as theirs must be the best. But I hope to prove to you that, in fact, all Jungian-based models are the same and even before Jung, the ancient Greeks, Romans, South Americans, and Chinese all had behavioral models akin to Jung's, but 3,000 or 4,000 years earlier. All we have done since the first one is rewrap the present in new paper. About 15 years ago, I cowrote *Spectrum*, with two colleagues, Steve Berry, who has written two books on strategy, and Dr. Jon Baber a specialist in leadership and high performing teams. The new model, which is based on color like many others, has several major features, advantages, and benefits over all the others. So, to comfort the ones wedded to other models and to all the academics out there, please know that any self-questionnaire model can be wrong as it is our opinion of ourselves or others. Yes, after you have done a few it can become the self-fulfilling prophecy and you will answer the questions with a mindset that I am one type, so I will answer as that type. But you know you, better than any academics do, better than any doctor, psychiatrist, or psychologist does, and so if you try to be honest and answer the questions as you are now, not as you want to be and not how you think others want you to be, it will, in 99 percent cases, give you a general style and flavor that is 90 percent like you and can help you to be more affective, more sensitive to situations, and able to influence and persuade others better so that you do not feel wounded, upset, or put upon, nor do you feel that you have had to get cross or sulk to get your way. I promise you it works. Please suspend your judgment until you have finished the whole book and then ask yourself—does this feel right, work, and is it basically a lot of common sense? Although I was told that the funny thing about common sense is that it isn't all that common!!

How difficult is it to change behavior? Easy, put someone into a stressful situation or put them in pain or illness and see them change behavior in seconds!

CHAPTER 2

Why Try or Even Consider a New Psychometric or Behavioral Assessment Tool?

For over 4,500 years we have studied behaviors from ancient Egypt to ancient Greek to the Roman Empire, the Chinese ancient culture, the Japanese culture, as well as South American Aztecs and Inca tribes, modern America, and across Africa. It has fascinated the learned and the average person going to work every day in a field. They have all asked the question: What is behavior? Many have come up with models and some of them are good and all have their place; some are dated and have strange labels but behind these labels is still the essence of a simple four-dimensional model that works as well today as it ever did. We must also add here that all the behavioral models that exist today are based on white middle class, often North American (USA) and Western cultural studies. We must allow for cultural differences between countries, regions, villages, tribes, and religions. Even the oldest behavioral and personality models (ancient Greece) and the modern protagonists of all known behavioral models in the 1950s where nearly all the models we have today started in the 1950s. There were an amazing number of Europeans and a high number of Jewish psychologists who studied behavior, and a lot of these went to the United States before, during, and after the Second World War. There are also some Russians, Polish, United Kingdom, and many Americans too, and many of these were looking at why some of the atrocities happened in Germany and my theory is that many became quite introspective studies of psychology, psychiatry, sociology, and behavior. Here are a few I have studied.

Galen—Turkish/Roman, Descartes—French, Herbart—German, Kier-
kegaard—Danish, Galton—English, Charcot—French, Kraepelin—
German, Wundt—German, James—United States, Hall—United States,
Ebbinghaus—German, Binet—French, Janet—French, Pavlov—Russian,
Thorndike—United States, Watson—United States, Tolman—United
States, Guthrie—United States, Lorenz—Austrian, Skinner—United
States, Wolpe—South Africa, Freud—Czech Republic and then Austria,
Adler—Austria, Fromm—German, Jung—Swiss, Klein—Austria,
Rogers—United States, Maslow—Russian/United States, Frankl—
Swiss, Kohler—German, Hebb—Canadian, Festinger—United States,
Ekmann—United States, Schacter—United States, Piaget—Swiss,
Bandura—Polish/Canadian, Chomsky—United States, Baron-Cohen—
England, Cattell—England, and Eysenck—Germany.

There are hundreds more. There are dozens of psychometric assessment tools out there with lie detectors built in and measures of how consistently you answer the same question twice, and they will give you a
valuable insight into people. We cannot change personality easily, but
we can influence and affect the important bit—behaviors. After all, we
cannot do much about our personalities, as they are set in stone; it is
difficult to change the cultures we live in; we have roles in our lives and
some come and go and many stay for our entire life times; and situations
are usually predictable but there are some that jump out and bite us. But
we can change our behaviors and we can then use these to get more from
others, be more efficient, maintain less conflict, and predict how someone
might behave and be ready. But what I found is that in each there is a
nugget of wisdom; in each something I could use or adapt and blend until
about 15 years ago three guys took the best of all the models out there,
created and challenged some of the accepted ones, and put together a new
perspective, and for 15 years it has been tried and tested without anyone
saying that is not me or it does not work. It was used on individuals to
help them understand their behaviors, and improve their effectiveness. It
can help you with leadership, presentations and public speaking, relationships at home and at work, sorting out issues and conflicts, selling, and
persuasion too.

It can help you become more inspirational, get on with people better, lead, be an effective team player, and be better at relationships in general. It could improve your ability to sell more and quicker; to work in project groups; to help them create identity, meaning, purpose, and direction; and to help them unblock blocks between teams and of course at the organizational level to look at the culture and how well the values are being lived by the staff.

These existing models use the same basic model for behavior—a four-style behavioral model. SPECTRUM is very similar but easier to understand, easier to remember, and more user friendly; you can alter and change your behaviors as simply as deciding you want to and we will show you how.

A lot of you will already be wedded to another model and yours will be the best. Like your favorite football team, designer you like wearing, or your political party, it is hard to change your beliefs, but what about having an alternative or an extra string to your bow rather than replacing yours? A complimentary affordable model that even the person who makes tea or sweeps the car park right up to the chief executive officer (CEO), vice president (VP), and senior directors and managers can easily understand and talk to each other about in the same language and understand what they both want? How can anyone understand "You are a introvert, Sensing, Feeling, and Judging (ISFJ) and I am a Extrovert, Intuitive, Feeling, and Perceiving (ETFP)" or "You are a conserving/holding on and I am an adapter/dealing away"? How can anyone remember it the next day, the next week, and then actually use it?

What if we said, that your preference is to use red behaviors and mine is to use yellow? You should instantly remember what each color means in behavioral terms and what motivates them and how to communicate with them. What do you think red behaviors are? What do you think yellow behaviors are? You are already right!

If you do not think this is true: I used Spectrum in a school with prefects aged 15. In 20 minutes, they had understood the model, built their own model, and changed the way they would deal with the other students because of seeing their role from another's perspective.

They thought they needed to be policemen, giving out detentions and lines and punishment for rule breaking—because that is how it has always been done. With 20 minutes of SPECTRUM training, they now treat the other students as customers, helping and supporting them and even buddying up with the year 7 students aged 11 to help them with homework and finding their way around the school, and getting advice and help on antibullying, and so on. A move from red and blue to green in 20 minutes.

But by Treating others as they want to be treated and it was found that incidents went down and there was less bullying and more helping nature and kindness instead of rules and regulations being adhered too.

Schools tend to use negative language and this reinforces the belief that it is a scary place to go for 5, 11, 16, and 18-year-olds, as they transition into new schools, colleges, and universities.

Here is one such rule—"Keep off the Grass!" (red). It has been replaced by "Please can all students try to keep to the footpaths (sidewalks) as walking on the grass when wet can kill it and make it very muddy. Thank you so much for being considerate!" (green & blue).

So, once you have a common language to use for behaviors and all are using the same one, you can talk to each other, you in their style and they in yours. But you can also use Spectrum to look at a team; a team can have a preference to use say Blue and the teams feeding into that team or receiving outputs from that team can better understand their needs. You can look at whole companies too; a Blue organization can understand that if they are selling to a yellow organization then safety, low cost, evidence of its success, and resale value do not matter to them; they prefer the latest, the best, the most innovative, and something that makes them look and feel good. One example of this is a company that decided to make a brand-new plastic Pandrol E clip for $1 (75p) each. For over 100 years London Transport had used a metal clip that cost $2 (£1.50). As a precaution, every third clip is replaced every five years so that there is a low chance of failure as every clip is changed every 15 years during maintenance. London Transport is a Blue organization. Uniforms; rules and regulations (by the book); timetables; and safety, health, and welfare of passengers are number one priority. The organization making the plastic clip was innovative, creative, and forward thinking, and tried to sell its clip first to London Transport by saying it was at half the price, lasted forever, and no one else had used it. Would you like to be first? Answer—No. After 20 years of selling this new clip around the world London Transport still has not committed to changing over. If they had approached ten others, with evidence of others' usage and safety and failure rates across three to five years they might have listened—they needed to treat their customer as the customer wanted to be treated, not as a a fast-moving, risk-taking, energetic, innovative organization—as they were at opposites in style. They did sell it in Australia, Japan, and other forward-thinking, fast-moving, and change-welcoming countries and organizations.

Here is a chart with my view of all the main players in behavior and psychometrics being used in the world today plus a few that have long since been lost to time.

Title / Author	Extrovert / Task	Extrovert / People	Introvert / People	Introvert / Task
Spectrum / Jarrett	RED	YELLOW	GREEN	BLUE
HIPPOCRATES & GALEN –370BC & 190AD	CHOLERIC	SANGUINE	PHLEGMATIC	MELANCHOLIC
ARISTOTLE -320BC	FIRE/WARM	AIR/COOL	WATER/MOIST	EARTH/DRY
JUNG FUNCTIONS	INTUITION	SENSATION	FEELING	THINKING
FROMM	TAKING	EXCHANGING	ACCEPTING	PRESERVING
KATCHER & ATKINS LIFO	CONTROLLING	ADAPTING	SUPPORTING	CONSERVING
MBTI – Myers-Briggs	EXTROVERT, THINKING, INTUITIVE, PERCEIVING	EXTROVERT, FEELING, SENSING, PERECEIVING	INTROVERT, FEELING, SENSING, JUDGING	INTROVERT, THINKING, INTUITIVE, JUDGING
JUNG – ATTITUDES	PERCEIVING, EXTERNALLY FOCUSED, OBJECTIVE	EXTROVERT, EXTERNALLY FOCUSED, SUBJECTIVE	JUDGING, INTERNALLY FOCUSED SUBJECTIVE	INTROVERT INTERNALLY FOCUSED OBJECTIVE
DISC – THOMAS INTERNATIONAL	DOMININANCE	INFLUENCE	CONSCIENTIOUSNESS	STAEDINESS
SDI	RED	MIX OF ALL THREE	BLUE	GREEN
WATSON & CRICK	ADRENINE	THYAMINE	CYTOSINE	GOANINE
PAVLOV	ENERGETIC	EXCITABLE	INHIBITED	STAEDFAST
IAN TIBBLES ACE	DRIVER	MIXER	HELPER	PLANNER
INSIGHTS	DIRECTOR/REFORMER	INSPIRER/MOTIVATOR	HELPER/SUPPORTER	COORDINATOR/ OBSERVER

FACET5	CONTROL/AGGRESSION	ENERGY/HAPPINESS	AFFECTION/SADNESS	WILL/PASSIVITY
PLATO 340BC	INTUITIVE	ARTISTIC	SENSIBLE	REASONED
MAR's Facial Shapes	OVAL	TRIANGULAR	ROUND	SQUARE
KEIRSEY	IDEALIST	ARTISAN	GUARDIAN	RATIONALIST
EMPEDOCLES	FIRE	AIR	EARTH	WATER
HIPPOCRATES	BLOOD	YELLOW BILE	PHLEGM	BLACK BILE
EYSENCK	RESTLESS	LIVELY	CAREFUL	RESERVED
BERZIGER	RESULTS	CREATIVITY	EMPATHY	ROUTINE
BIG 5	EXTROVERT CONFIDENT	EXTROVERT CREATIVE	INTROVERT SENSITIVE	INTROVERT DETAIL
BIRKMAN	AUTHORITY	ACTIVITY	ACCEPTANCE	STRUCTURE
OPQ	EXTROVERT TASK FOCUSED	EXTROVERT PEOPLE FOCUSED	INTROVERT PEOPLE FOCUSED	INTROVERT TASK FOCUSED

Exercise to compare your preferred model to Spectrum

Put down the features, advantages, and benefits of your preferred model if you have one and then when you have finished the book come back to this page and see how many you can tick off that Spectrum can also do. Be fair and be honest.

Name of your preferred behavioral model?	Features of this model? (What does it do?)	Advantages of this model (Why is it better than other models?)	Benefits of this model?	Does Spectrum have this? Yes in all cases!!

CHAPTER 3

The Formula & What Is Personality (Basic Understanding)

Let us start with a simple formula [adapted from *Managing Your Strengths* by Allan Katcher (2002), *The Name of Your Game* by Dr. Stuart Atkins (1981), *Man for Himself* by Erich Fromm (1947), and *Client Centered Therapy* by Carl R. Rodgers (1951)].

$$\frac{P \times S}{R + C} = B$$

P = Personality
S = Situations
R = Role
C = Culture
B = Behavior

The formula conveys that your personality reacts with any given situation and is affected by the role you are playing at that time and the culture you are in to create a behavior.

What is Personality?—we all have a personality? One of the most commonly accepted models is Type A and Type B, as created by Mayer Friedman and Ray Rosenman, two cardiologists who looked at the risks of coronary disease based on two personality types. Saville and Holdsworth's Organizational Personality Questionnaires (OPQ) tests, which are used the most in the Western world today, are based on the four-paradigm model, which accounts for 95 percent of the known models. The OPQ measures 32 different personality traits that are relevant to occupational settings. Ultimately, the tests measure traits with the purpose of determining your behavioral style at work. Employers often use this personality test to see how good job applicants fit the role they are applying for. When undertaking the OPQ, you are asked to make forced-choice responses (otherwise referred to as an ipsative approach, where you have to choose one answer). For instance, each question in the OPQ has four statements or adjectives such as friendly, leader, team player, and confident. You are required to rate which are the most and least like you out of the four statements/adjectives, rather than rating each individual statement or adjective on a scale. Thus, your final score is likely to indicate your relative strengths and weaknesses. It is therefore important to prepare for such tests through online-practice psychometric tests so that you are confident that you are demonstrating your strengths to your potential employer when you undertake your real psychometric test.

There are 32 personality traits measured in the OPQ and are grouped into categories such as: Relationships, Sociability (e.g., outgoing, socially confident), Influence (e.g., persuasive, outspoken, independent minded), Empathy (e.g., democratic, caring), and Thinking style (e.g., evaluative, rational). The OPQ also includes a social desirability measure to detect *faking* responses. The multidimensional forced-choice nature of the OPQ can be cognitively challenging for test takers. For instance, processing several items at the same time requires good reading skills and comprehension. Additionally, choosing which statement is most and least like you requires you to conduct several mental comparisons that can be stressful when you are under pressure and the stakes are high. This highlights the benefits of practicing psychometric tests online.

There is also the NEOAC–Big Five, which says that there are five parts to personality—N = need for stability: low, medium, or high; E = extraversion to introversion levels; O = originality and openness; A = accommodation, agreeableness, and adaptability; and C = consolidation and conscientiousness.

We like the *Type A or Type B* as defined in most models but instead of choosing one answer we say that you can be anywhere between the two continua—and this in very simple terms defines your personality as who you are. The deep stuff, inside your head and which cannot be seen, and there is some stuff in there that you do not even know about yourself or certainly do not want others to see. I will talk about level A and level B a bit deeper later.

Personality is, for me, who you are, what makes you tick, what motivates you, your values and beliefs, and your ethos and spirit. The deep, inner structure of your brain, your ancestry, and your morals are mostly inherited, learned, developed, and evolved, but are affected by the environment; what is around you; how you are brought up; where you live in the world; and your level of wealth, health, and education.

Let me use a computer analogy. Most of us can use a computer to differing levels of competence—similar to that, we all use behaviors to differing levels of effectiveness.

Behavior is what we see and hear just like that; what appears on the screen of a computer or comes out of the printer is the behavior. Few of us understand the software and hardware, nor want to. Just like behavior, it is on the surface, what can be seen and heard, but the software and all the hardware are like our body, brains, and our personalities—deep and hidden.

Without reading a whole book on personality, others are better qualified to explain these theories; I want to simplify it but if you want to read more on personality theories I have suggested some further reading.

Here is a simple way to begin to understand our personalities.

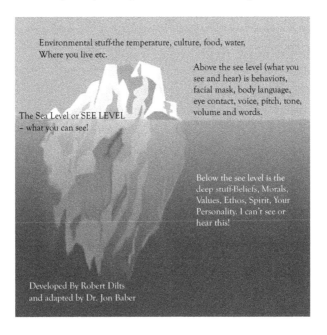

Environmental stuff-the temperature, culture, food, water, Where you live etc.

Above the see level (what you see and hear) is behaviors, facial mask, body language, eye contact, voice, pitch, tone, volume and words.

The Sea Level or SEE LEVEL - what you can see!

Below the see level is the deep stuff-Beliefs, Morals, Values, Ethos, Spirit, Your Personality. I can't see or hear this!

Developed By Robert Dilts and adapted by Dr. Jon Baber

Personality is the deeper stuff: values, beliefs, morals, culture, and traits inherited from all your gene pool, parents, grandparents, and so on; the environmental influences from birth to death; your careers; your education and upbringing; your life experiences, both bad and good; and levels of health.

Ninety percent of the iceberg is below the sea level and only 10 percent above; change the sea to see—what we can observe and what we cannot could be related to our personality. The bit above the sea or *see* level is what we can see and the bit below is hidden just like our personality. What would be above *your see* level? Your behavior is a window to your personality and the bit that can be seen. What is hidden and what shows?

Behavior is above the *see* level—we can observe behavior. Capabilities and work-based and home-based competences and skills too are above the *see* level.

However, the environment is outside the iceberg but has an influence on it, through temperature change and weather, which can affect the iceberg in the same way in which other people, laws, culture, education, and more important life experiences could affect your personality. Are you the same person after a close family member dies?

Beliefs and values could be close to or on the surface and may be hidden or showing depending on who you are, who you are with, and how introvert or extrovert you are. Your morals and levels of introvert and extrovert nature, goals, and ambition could also show.

The deep stuff is your spirit, ethos, and identity—you may keep this secretive from others and even yourself—it is private. The longer you know someone, the more the *see level* might move down and you might reveal more of the deeper personality. Marry them and you could get even deeper but there will always be bits of your own personality that is hidden from everyone and even some of theirs is hidden from you.

The more extrovert you are, the lower the *see* level, and the more introvert you are, the higher the *see* level. Extroverts tend to show you more than introverts. Friedman explains Type A and Type B personalities as follows.

Type A

The theory describes Type A individuals as ambitious, rigidly organized, highly status conscious, sensitive, impatient, anxious, proactive, and concerned with time management. People with Type A personalities are often high-achieving *workaholics*. They push themselves with deadlines, and hate both delays and ambivalence.

In his 1996 book dealing with extreme Type A behavior, *Type A Behavior: Its Diagnosis and Treatment*, Friedman suggests that dangerous Type A behavior is expressed through three major symptoms: (1) free-floating hostility, which can be triggered by even minor incidents; (2) time urgency and impatience, which cause irritation and exasperation usually described as being *short-fused*; and (3) a competitive drive, which causes stress and an achievement-driven mentality. The first of these symptoms is believed to be covert and therefore less observable, while the other two are more overt.

Type B

The theory describes Type B individuals as a contrast to those of Type A. Type B personalities are noted to live at lower stress levels. They typically work steadily, and may enjoy achievement, although they have a greater tendency to disregard physical or mental stress when they do not achieve. When faced with competition, they may focus less on winning or losing than their Type A counterparts, and more on enjoying the game regardless of winning or losing. Unlike the Type A personality's rhythm of multitasking careers, Type B individuals are sometimes attracted to careers of creativity: writer, counsellor, therapist, actor, or actress. However, network and computer system managers, professors, and judges are more likely to be Type B individuals as well. Their personal character may enjoy exploring ideas and concepts. They are often reflective, and think of the *outer and inner world*.

OPQ (Saville and Holdsworth) is one of the widest used and probably the best personality tests in the world and is often used for aptitude tests, determining suitability for employment, promotion to very high-level jobs, and many other aspects. It is excellent. There is also NEOAC and the Big Five Personality factors—from "Personality at Work" by Howard and Howard, which is a five-paradigm model, again excellent and worth looking at, but you need to be a level A– and level B–qualified expert to interpret the data; so that excludes 99 percent of the population. I wanted something that you could do at home, without expert help. I am not knocking or criticizing personality profiling tools and techniques; it is just that we have all excluded everyone unless we have £150 ($200) to spend on it or £1,000 ($1,500) to spend on a therapist.

So, we have taken a brief and shallow look at personality, and given some references where you might explore this further; situations are dynamic and too many to talk about other than to say that every second of every day the situation changes and may require you to change the hat you are wearing (role you are playing) and require a different piece of behavior. There are hundreds of books on personality—this is not a book about personality or psychology, but just about how I see how your personality may interact with your behaviors to create a style that is unique to you. Finally, remember that personality is deep and we cannot see it; you need to live with someone for years to begin to understand their personality, but you can change behavior in a moment without changing your values or beliefs. Try smiling now; you have just changed your behavior without changing your personality and, guess what, it probably made you have positive feelings, because as we smile, it makes us feel better and happier even if just for a moment. We train people in call centers, and we always say smile when on the phone because the other person can hear a smile and it is true.

But what if instead of being either a Type A or a Type B personality, it was a continuum. What if it was a scale from say +10 to 0 to −10 = or from very extrovert, medium extroversion or low extroversion or highly introvert, or medium or low introversion? What if you could say about yourself—I am quite extrovert but not totally, or a bit introvert but not extremely, or, as I have found with many people, neither extrovert nor introvert but somewhere in the middle.

I like to simplify it; so personality comes from four areas that are not equal, vary from person to person, are unique to you, and can all change if an individual has long-term changes to his or her life: levels of health, illness, and fitness, and a change in a role; being promoted or demoted or relationship; divorce or death of a relative or friend or environment; prison, change of country, county, city, town, village, or rural or urban changes too; and moving house could also change your personality. If one thing changes, everything changes. Here are a few things that may affect your personality for the longer term and are harder to change once set. To what degree are you affected? If you place your mark between the two ends of the SPECTRUM, you can start building your own personality profile.

Introvert	Extrovert
Intelligence inherited Low	High
Intelligence Learned in first 18-25 years low	High
Internally focused on self & thinking	Externally on outside world
Long Term Planning	Short Team
Intuition	Planned
Emotional	Rational
Serious	Humorous
Outside looking in	Inside looking out
Impulsive	Thought Out
Sporty/Competitive	Uncompetitive/Solo e.g. - Book Worm
Active	Passive
Participatory	Non-Participatory
Risk Taking	Safety
Charismatic	Staid
Practical	Clumsy
Creative (fron scratch/new)	Innovative (change the existing)
Friendly	Anti-Social
Highly Sexual	Frigid
Faithful/Loyal	Disloyal/Unfaithful
Helpful	Selfish
Peaceful	Aggressive
Stable/Steady	Unstable/Excitable

Inherited Traits

1. Inherited (what you are born with)—*NATURE*: Naturally, through your genetic pool handed to you in your DNA from your natural mother and father and all your ancestors. So, sorry, whether you like it or not, you are going to be like your mother and father not only in looks, but also personality traits and their behaviors. So, when your parents told you off for being too loud, too excitable or sulky, you were probably copying them. So some of your personality is set in stone at birth and in your early years—post- and antenatal and certainly by your teenage years.

2. Environmental (what affects the roles we play, the situations we find ourselves in, and surroundings we live in)—*NURTURE*: How and where you were brought up, including the effects other family members have on you, the community you live in, and your friends all had on you. The education you received is paramount and can affect your values, beliefs, and morals. This is usually set by the time you have reached adulthood. So, your values and your beliefs can be set quite early in your life and can be based on the environment you were brought up in. For example, a privileged upbringing with money versus a tough life in a working class suburb.

3. Learned (what we learn from birth to death)—*NURTURE*: Anything you have been taught, coached, mentored, trained, or have taught yourself goes in to making us who we are—local sayings and accents, expressions, and copying your role models.

4. Evolving (what we choose to do with our lives, health levels, relationships, careers, and life experiences)—*NURTURE* and *NATURE*—accidents and deliberates: Personality traits that evolve and change from the day you are born to the day you die (and possibly beyond) affected by education, career, marriage, children, life experiences, death of loved ones, severe illness, life changes, moving home, even holidays, and so on.

What Can Change Your Personality?

There are permanent and temporary changes to your life that can affect your personality or behavior or both. Your personality is as solid as the ground you walk on; it does not change much or often but there are natural and unnatural events that can change the ground we walk on for us. I compare permanent changes to the ground we walk on to an earthquake and temporary changes to a digger digging up the ground we walk on and then putting it back nearly like it was before.

Permanent changes could be the death of a loved one, which could affect any number of aspects of your personality, temporarily or forever.

Prior to my stepfather's death, my mother was more extrovert than introvert, enjoying parties, social occasions, pubs, noise, and being with others, and had little or no religious beliefs, certainly none that was on show and she certainly rarely went to church.

When my stepfather Michael died, my mother had a permanent change to her life, an earthquake. Initially, her behaviors changed as you would expect but because these changes were forever, she became more introvert, and over two to three years she became more religious. Now she is rarely seen in a pub, or with groups, preferring to be on a one-to-one basis with people or even being left alone. She goes to church and outwardly states her new beliefs. Her personality had changed forever and so had her behaviors. Change the software or hardware and what you get on screen changes.

A career change could also change your behavior and possibly your personality; think of a second-hand car salesman, who becomes a bereavement counsellor, or you becoming a prison warden for the rest of your working life. Initially, you would get some behavioral changes like being more thorough, careful, and methodical, but eventually you might get some personality changes, which are permanent such as a move from being extrovert to introvert. So, behavioral changes in the short term become personality changes in the long term.

All these changes can be affected by those who had expectations of this person, what they expected, what role they were playing & in what situation they are in now and how well they met that expectation.

So, we must also consider situations—there are millions of situations: the phone rings, the doorbell chimes, a letter arrives, an e-mail arrives, an emergency situation occurs, or any number of other situations you can think of at work, at home, with friends, or in sport.

Then we must also look at the roles we play—this is equal to the role, the culture, and so you could be the boss, a subordinate, a customer, a supplier, a mother or father, a brother or a sister, a friend, a colleague, a peer, a relative, or a salesperson, and when they interact with you, you change your behavior based on your role, their roles, and the current situation.

Culture is another influencer of how we behave—it is affected by the outside world, and influenced by where you are. This could the country, the region, the religion you believe in or not, the street you live or lived in, the organizational culture you work in, the social group you have, and so on. This creates changing levels of eye contact—from high or strong eye contact to low or no eye contact, the body language can be open—hands showing arms by side leaning in toward the other person or to a closed body language where the head is turned away and the arms folded and the person is trying to create distance between themselves and the other person. And also the facial mask being used (some people say facial expressions—smiling, serious, staring at or away, head down or up and so on) combine all these with a high to low pitch, tone, volume, and obviously, the content (what you say) and we receive all these four things and decide what behaviors are being used and are they congruent? By congruent I mean do they match in all parts of behavior giving me the same message? Is the voice pitch tone and volume matching the body language and facial mask being used—is it clear? This is huge and affects how good we are at communication. We are not as good today as we were even 100 years ago at using our faces and voice and bodies to communicate clearly to others, mainly because of the invention of the phone, then mobiles, (cell phones) and computers, we now only use one of these at a time to communicate to others. So, phones—voice pitch tone and volume only no body language or face. E-mail and text-content only—and how we behave is directly affected by Cultures we live in. Think of the increase in the use emojis to let others know how we are feeling!

In the *People Management* magazine published in October 2016, there was an article by Jane Simms on cultural misunderstandings, in which she covered some core human resources (HR) issues from around the world and how these affected people's behaviors.

Brazil—most municipalities forbid the use of mobile phones inside banking agencies, to protect bank users from being robbed on exiting the building. This radically changed the behavior of customers.

United States—it is illegal to fire an employee because they are lesbian, gay, bisexual, or transgender in 29 states. This radically changed the behavior of people searching for work and truly revealed who they were.

Italy—in Milan, it is a legal requirement to smile always—except during funerals and hospital visits. This radically changed the way people behave.

China—as part of a public policy to encourage marriage and child-birth later in life, the government gave people over 30, time off work to marry and procreate, and if they had a baby nine months later, they received benefits from the state. This was written in legislation in some Chinese provinces; again this radically changed the way people behaved.

Russia—couples in the region of Ulyanovsk are given the day off on September 12 to procreate, and they could win cash prizes if they have children nine months later. Again, this radically changed the way people behaved.

United Kingdom—people used to be required to see a doctor after two days of sickness to get a certificate for their employers to prove it and the average time off work then was less than two days. It was changed to seven days before you needed to see a doctor to get the same certificate and now the average time off work has increased. This changed the way we behave.

Amongst the many African tribes, there are three tribes (Nandi, Kipsigis, and Maasii): one, where it is seen to be great if you are manly and very aggressive, another where passivity is rewarded, and a third where a drug is used to turn passivity into aggression.

We must also consider our own cultural (local) thermometer and those of others, to allow for more aggressive societies or speed of language (Arabic), or animated body language (Latin), or the volume of voice (USA), or greetings, which include kissing (France), touching (Italy), and so on, we need to be considerate and tolerant of other people's cultures and not just imposing ours on them. If it is culturally accepted to cover your arms, then cover them. In other words, *treat others as they want to be treated.* We have more in common than that which divides us and yet we fight over the tiny bits that we disagree over. The Christians and the Muslims, the Roman Catholics and the Protestants, your football team versus my football team bring us to blows and acts of violence. What we believe and value will cause violence despite having 95 percent in common with the person next to us. What we see as strength in the United Kingdom might be seen by another society/culture/country/region or even organization as a weakness, and vice versa. The Buddhists are passive, and so is the Tantric way of life; the Muslims have some aggressive sects in the

Sunnis and Shiites and passive ones in the Druze, Alawi, Ismaili, and Sufi Wahhabi, and so do the Jews who can be passive or aggressive to extremes—take Jewish behavior in the concentration camps where tens of thousands would be controlled by a few Nazi soldiers without fighting back or trying to escape and the aggressive way in which the Israelis are fighting with Palestinians. We have passive factions and aggressive wings; in the United Kingdom, with BMP, NF, and the mainstream parties, even trade unions can be *militant*. Christians have been fighting each other since one man was nailed to a cross for saying, "Why don't we all live together equally and in peace?" Some trade unions are more aggressive than others and some world leaders are too. Think of George Bush Junior, Ronald Reagan, Donald Trump, Mahmoud Ahmadinejad, Hamid Karzai, Vladimir Putin, Kim Jong Un, and Bashar-al Assad and how their behaviors can affect how nations think, feel, and behave. Now think of your boss, chief executive officer (CEO), managing director (MD), vice president (VP), team leader, or manager in the team in which you work, and now tell me they do not set the standards of behavior, culture, and ethos of your team—time keeping, dress code, and what is acceptable or not in your subculture. Your boss/managers are only as good as the standard they walk by and ignore or do something about.

Culture also affects our community and personal values, and these values affect our behavior. There are great books on culture, values, religion, beliefs, and psychology, but again this is not what we are trying to teach you.

So, let us now assume that in general terms we have a basic handle on our personality, which includes our values and beliefs; the culture we live and work in; and the roles that we play, whether it is a father, mother, brother, sister, son, daughter, boss, subordinate, customer, supplier, peer etc. and acknowledge that every day, the situation is constantly changing. An incoming phone call, an e-mail, a meeting, a conversation, a letter, or a comment from a colleague or friend can affect our responding behaviors and influence how we feel. Let us look more deeply at behavior and how stress and changing situations can affect the way we behave. I do honestly believe that we are generally trying to be positive and create a good outcome, but the way we try to achieve it and the behaviors we display cause all the blocks, all the clashes, and all the frustration we have with another person, team, or department.

Exercise—Try and Plot Your Basic Personality Profile and Ask Others How Like You, It Really Is? Talk It Through with a Trusted Friend.

Introvert	Extrovert
Intelligence inherited Low	High
Intelligence Learned in first 18–25 years low	High
Internally focused on self & thinking	Externally on outside world
Long Term Planning	Short Team
Intuition	Planned
Emotional	Rational
Serious	Humorous
Outside looking in	Inside looking out
Impulsive	Thought Out
Sporty/Competitive	Uncompetitive/Solo e.g. - Book Worm
Active	Passive
Participatory	Non-Participatory
Risk Taking	Safety
Charismatic	Staid
Practical	Clumsy
Creative (fron scratch/new)	Innovative (change the existing)
Friendly	Anti-Social
Highly Sexual	Frigid
Faithful/Loyal	Disloyal/Unfaithful
Helpful	Selfish
Peaceful	Aggressive
Stable/Steady	Unstable/Excitable

Notes

Exercise—think about the common situations you find yourself in every-day and then write down some situations that were new to you or were out of your comfort zone or had never been in before, and write down how you felt when in control of situations and when you were not in control.

Write down some of the common and well known situations that you are often in? and how you felt at the time?	Situations you found yourself in but wasn't prepared or ready? And how you felt?
For example, watching TV, Working - relaxed, carefree	Getting Married for first time!, nervous, worried, stressed, excited and out of control!!

Exercise—Describe the Main Roles You Have in Your Life Today Using a Domanial Map and What Uniquely Do They Expect of You? Here Is Mine.

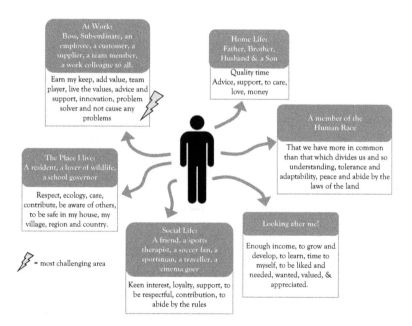

At Work:
Boss, Sub-ordinate, an employee, a customer, a supplier, a team member, a work colleague to all.

Earn my keep, add value, team player, live the values, advice and support, innovation, problem solver and not cause any problems

Home Life:
Father, Brother, Husband & a Son

Quality time
Advice, support, to care, love, money

A member of the Human Race

That we have more in common than that which divides us and so understanding, tolerance and adaptability, peace and abide by the laws of the land

The Place I live:
A resident, a lover of wildlife, a school governor

Respect, ecology, care, contribute, be aware of others, to be safe in my house, my village, region and country.

⚡ = most challenging area

Social Life:
A friend, a sports therapist, a soccer fan, a sportsman, a traveller, a cinema goer

Keen interest, loyalty, support, to be respectful, contribution, to abide by the rules

Looking after me!

Enough income, to grow and develop, to learn, time to myself, to be liked and needed, wanted, valued, & appreciated.

Now do yours. Which one do you find the most challenging?

Exercise—Describe the Culture You Live in—Try This to Help You. Adapted from "New Media and Cultural Identity"—Chinese Media Research (2006).

- Location—where do you live?
  - Which part of the world?
  - Which country?
  - Which region?
  - Which city?
  - Which town?
  - Which village?
  - Which area?
  - Which street?
  - Which house?
- What sex are you?
- Think about your history
  - Where have you come from?
  - Early life and upbringing
  - Ancestry: all about your deep routes
- Nationality
- Languages you speak
- Religious beliefs that affect your daily life—if any
- Ethnicity
- What possessions you have around you?
- What do you eat and drink?
- Where do you work?
- Journey to work
- Infrastructure and travel
- Hospitals and health care
- Schools and education
- Friends and neighbors

There are more but this will get you started and begin the conversation about how much does culture play a part in our behaviors.

CHAPTER 4

What Is Behavior?

There is a myth that behavior is something that is difficult to understand and difficult to change or influence; that you need to be an academic; have a degree in psychology or psychiatry; or be a life coach, a therapist, or a qualified counsellor. But no. You know yourself, better than anyone else, all you need is a code, a model, or a system to use which is simple and unforgettable.

Guess what we are; we are already experts but we have forgotten to use the skills we were given; ancient man had a sensing mechanism for danger, lust, hunger, thirst, and so on, and he had developed these to be heightened so that he could know minutes before he was in danger, that danger was near—we have lost this ability as it has become atrophied and dormant. People now walk into the path of a car with their smart devices and headphones on, unaware of the dangers; Stone Age man could sense a threat from miles away. We still can but only if we exercise and work the human brain, the most powerful computer in the known universe and yet some say we only use 5 percent on a good day. Let us start becoming more aware again of others' eyes and facial expressions, read body language, and really tune into ourselves and others quickly, accurately and with a strategy to deal with almost any situation.

Human Behavior Poem—anon (also released as a song by Bjork, 1993):

If you ever get close to a human
and human behavior
Be ready, be ready to get confused

There's definitely, definitely, no logic
to human behavior
But yet so, yet so irresistible
And there's no map

They're terribly moody
and human behavior
Then all of a sudden turn happy

But, oh, to get involved in the exchange
of human emotions
Is ever so, ever so satisfying

Oh oh, and there's no map

Human behavior, human
Human, human behavior, human
Human, human behavior, human
Human behavior, human

And there's no map
And the compass
Wouldn't help at all

Human behavior, human, human
Human behavior, human
Human behavior, human
Human behavior

There's definitely, definitely, definitely no logic

Well I think she is wrong. There is a map and there is a compass and there is some logic.

We have preconceived ideas about behavior and personality and yet how many of us know what behavior is and what personality is. But we have lost the deeper ability to see what color the other person is, what motivates them, what color we are and what motivates us, and then to find common ground and to sell the common ground in their style, their language, with their facial mask, pitch, tone, and volume, and use words that they like to hear such as to be asked to do something rather than told. If we can get this right, if we can unlock the other person, we can then persuade them to do something, sell to them, buy from them, lead them, work with them, and yes even have a long-lasting relationship. It could even lead to understanding your children.

Behavior: In my opinion behavior is how you communicate with yourself (inner dialogue) and others (outer dialogue) and it is nothing more than:

What we say—the words that you use
How we say it—what pitch, what tone, and what volume

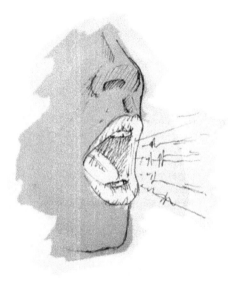

The facial expressions we use—the eye contact and eye movement that accompanies the facial expressions: smile, grimace, pain, happiness, affection, worry, stress, and so on.

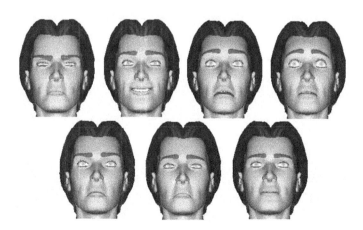

Body language—how you stand or sit, what you do with your limbs, body, and head. We call this your shape or look: animation and use of limbs and body shape.

Now, the secret is to get your voice, body, and face to be congruent—in line with each other—in other words, if you display the appropriate language, pitch, tone, volume, facial mask, and body language for any given situation then you are an excellent communicator, but if you don't, others will misread your behavior and you might get some strange reactions from others leading to conflict and stressful situations.

WYSIWYG—what you see is what you get

How you use your words and pitch tone and volume is within your control and can be changed, and this was superbly put in *Change your Voice, Change your Life* by Dr. Morton Cooper, who in 1984 said that the voice chamber in your mouth can be both physically changed through physiotherapy and exercises to change the pitch and tone, as can breathing and lungs and muscles in the chest to change volumes. It can be done and I did it and so can you.

Your body language and face can then be changed to match your voice or vice versa. We can learn again to use better posture, facial expressions, and eye contact to get what we want or to mirror others through observation and practice as described in another great book, *Body Language* by

Allan Pease (1981), and *The Psychology of Facial Expression* by James A. Russell and Jose Miguel Fernandez-Dols (1997). These books describe in detail how to use your face, eyes, and body, and moreover to read body language. More recently, Neuro Linguistic Programming (NLP) techniques, especially in a book called *NLP at Work*, Sue Knight even describes eye mapping and how and where you look when trying to recall something real or construct something new; your eyes will dart in different directions to show others whether you are constructing something (maybe even lying) or remembering something (maybe telling the truth). So, remember when looking at someone they can see into your soul. Watch children when they lie and see where they look—it won't be at you.

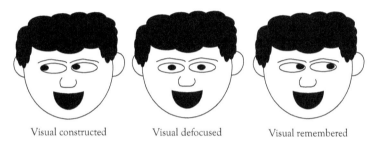

Visual constructed   Visual defocused   Visual remembered

No matter how hard they try they cannot look into your eyes when lying, and as we get older we get better but still find this difficult; so when you are late for work and use "traffic was bad" as an excuse, just remember that some people can read your eyes like others can read words on a page and know you may not be telling the truth. The standard map for this is as follows, but please remember that we are all unique and have our own maps and so you need to ask a few control questions first to unpick their map.

Exercise—Try asking one of your friends to think of a pink fluffy Rolls Royce outside waiting to take you home—get them to describe it to you and see which way they glance. They are making this up/constructing it. And for remembered things, ask them to tell you about the best holiday they ever had and describe what it was like there and what they did. Again, look at where they glance: Is this remembered or the truth as they remember it? I promise that their eyes will at some stage glance in a direction as the optic nerve connects with the brain and an involuntary muscle spasm makes their eyes glance up or left or right or down. Try not to tell them too much or else they might try and stare you out. Then ask another question to see if they are lying or not: Did you ever steal sweets from a sweet shop?

So, are you an effective communicator? How often do others not understand what you have just said or wanted from them? Do you get cross more than you should? Where your frustration of others not understanding you, or doing what you said, turns into anger? Do you get frustrated and feel let down more often than others? How often do you turn away and think, forget it, I will do it myself, I can't be bothered? Are you a sulker? Do you become quiet and uncommunicative? Or maybe you are a comedian in many normal and stressful situations trying to lighten the atmosphere? No one takes you seriously and you get laughed at when you are trying to be serious? Do you prefer to be alone or in company or maybe a bit of both depending on the day, the time, the mood, the moment, or what has just happened? Do people often misunderstand you? Do they get the wrong end of the stick and jump down your throat or get cross with you when your intention was not to do this? Are there some people who you find "easier" to get on with you than others? Are you sarcastic? You may find that your family, your friends, and work colleagues all find you slightly different; all see you as a different person or maybe a WYSIWYG? What you see is what you get. Are you a steady Eddie—someone who never changes regardless of situation, role, or environment? What about the situation in which you are under pressure or stressed? Do you change a lot or not much at all?

If you could simply identify your preferred style in normal situations and in stressful situations and then identify the triggers that cause you to over- or underreact in any given situation and find alternative strategies that work, you would become a more effective person in all situations, wouldn't you? Well, SPECTRUM can.

> Anyone can become angry—that is easy. But to be angry with the right person, to the right degree, at the right time, for the right purpose, and in the right way—this is not easy. (Aristotle 350 BC)

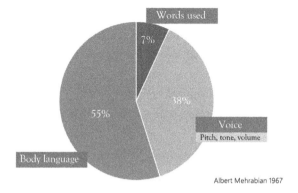

Albert Mehrabian 1967

Approximately 80 percent of communication is nonverbal (body, face, and eyes) and 15 percent the tune (pitch, tone, and volume), and only 5 percent the content. To prove this, say the following sentences but read the underlined bold words louder and emphasize more than the rest of the sentence, which you should read in a monotone voice. Imagine that the police are interviewing seven witnesses who all say the same sentence (content) but emphasize a different word each time. What conclusion would the police have about the whole story?

> **_I_** never said she stole my wallet—leaving the police to think that "I" didn't say this, it was someone else who said it.
>
> I **_never_** said she stole my wallet—leaving the police to think that I have never actually said this in the first place.
>
> I never **_said_** she stole my wallet—leaving the police to think that I may have implied it in writing; or some other way—but didn't say it.
>
> I never said **_she_** stole my wallet—leaving the police to think they may have the wrong suspect.
>
> I never said she **_stole_** my wallet—leaving the police to think that she didn't steal it, but was looking after it or believed she had permission in some way.
>
> I never said she stole **_my_** wallet—leaving the police to think that the wallet is not even yours or it was someone else's that was stolen.
>
> I never said she stole my **_wallet_**—leaving the police to think that it isn't even a wallet that was stolen.

So, watch out. Texting and E-mailing are dangerous—I once sent a text to five friends whom I was due to meet after work for a drink—saying "I am not coming now!" Each one of my friends responded as follows:

1st person—Why are you not coming?

2nd person—So what time will you be here? How late? Shall we wait for you?

3rd person—Who has upset you? What did they say to make you not want to come?

4th person—Who IS coming then? Are you bringing someone with you?

5th person—Have you had a shit day at work? What happened? #Busyday #shithappens!

I had broken down in my car and was waiting for the RAC (emergency breakdown services) to arrive; so no one got the right message and whose fault was it that they all misunderstood me?

Exercise—read the "I never said she/he stole my wallet" to a friend and emphasize each word underlined and ask them to tell you what they think you mean?

So what is behavior?

The dictionary says it is, "the way in which one acts or conducts oneself, especially toward others." and the Thesaurus says, "conduct, way of behaving, way of acting, deportment, bearing and etiquette, actions, efforts, manners, habits and practices, performance, operation, working methods, reaction & response."

I believe and would like to offer a new meaning for behavior as I have already stated: Behavior is the output or communication style you use to get your message across to others, to influence, to lead, to sell, to coach, to teach, to entertain, to join in, and it is simply your voice; content, pitch, tone, and volume; together with your facial mask and body language.

If your voice pitch, tone, and volume; facial mask; and body language are congruent—the same or matching—with your intention, you are good at using your behavior and if not then you could do with improving your communication style. Adjust your voice content—the words you use or the volume or the pitch or the tone—your body language, or your facial expressions to make you more effective and easier to read.

Words, pitch, tone, and volume are self-explanatory and the content is the words you use, the actual language, how loud you speak, and intonation and expression that you use.

Your facial expression is mainly concerned with your eye contact and how and where you focus, the angle of your head, and the way you use the muscles in your face and mouth to express yourself.

Body Language is how you use your body to get close to or away from someone else; how you stand, sit, and walk; and how you move and use your arms in gestures. It is believed that 80 percent of your communication is seen in the body language and facial mask.

Combine the three together and you have behavior, which is then received and interpreted as your behavioral style, and we tend to judge these behaviors often using negative language such as, "Tosser," "Idiot," "Fool," "Clown," "Stubborn," "Arrogant," "Sulky," "Miserable," "Twit," and so on. But what does that mean?

Sometimes we use even more positive language but still does not help us to explore the intention behind the behavior, such "he's lovely," "she's sweet," "he is kind and helpful," "she is funny," and so on. And by the way, we mostly use negative language and rarely use positive language to describe others.

If a parent or role model (a teacher) uses negative language on a child just once—it can last forever. My art teacher once tore my artwork to pieces in front of the class and made me feel so bad that I never tried to draw again—stating I cannot draw. But when did I learn NOT to draw. You will all have heard people say, "I can't sing, can't tell jokes, can't dance, can't play a sport etc." But it is not that they can't, it is that they have been told they can't or failed once at it and they believed this and stored this self-limiting belief forever. And remember a belief is simply something you perceive to be true without all the proof. Religious beliefs, the tooth fairy, and Father Christmas are examples of beliefs without proof.

There was a little girl in a classroom aged three who had NO self-limiting beliefs, and when I asked her what she was painting she said it is GOD. So, I said no one knows what God looks like. And her reply was simple, "If you wait a minute until I have finished you will find out what God looks like."

The next time someone uses negative language on you try this— "when did you learn NOT to be able to (paint, sing, dance, or drive) (or whatever they are being negative about)." And they cannot answer easily. Whether you believe you can or can't do something you are right, whether you believe you are right or wrong, you have already self-limited your ability to change by putting up a barrier.

How we communicate relies mainly on body language, including face and eyes; then the pitch, tone, volume, or musical tune of our voices; and last is the actual words, so written is least effective. If you do not believe me, watch a film with the sound down or in a foreign language and you will understand everything that is going on without subtitle.

This book covers all the basics about behavior, in a simple way that the guy who empties your trash or the man who runs the largest blue chip company can easily and quickly understand and talk to each in the SAME LANGUAGE and in summary—or in short hand and it doesn't matter, that you haven't got a degree in psychology or read 25 technical books on behavior and personality or studied psychometrics.

If his preference is red behaviors, and I act and respond to those needs and wants, he will like and appreciate me more but if I don't there is a risk that there will be a clash and one of us will feel wounded in some way after the experience. So, if Mr. Red says, "I want this report now" and I do my best to give it to him now, or Mrs. Green says, "I want this report to look great and I make it look great," or Mr. Yellow says, "I need this report to include everyone's views and opinions and make it an innovative document not dull and boring." I do just that. If Mr. Blue says "check it twice, proof read it for errors, make sure the facts are right, and that everything has been included," and I do this, each one of my managers is satisfied.

From its theatrical roots in ancient Greece, Egypt, and the Rome, to the twenty-first-century behavioral models like SPECTRUM, which I think is the newest, behavior has been spoken about and debated by the greatest minds ever, but in simple terms, it remains to be who you are (personality), and then what you do (behaviors)—the what you do, which clearly defines you as a person to others, not so much your personality.

I have tried to use brief summaries of the main players in some of the other theoretical models of personality and behavior that are on the market today, all of which are great, but tend to be very expensive, use complicated words, which no one can remember the next day, and moreover, no one can even use the next day. They are neither practical nor memorable. So, let me tell what Spectrum is now and then I will use the rest of the book to justify it and prove it to you.

Your personality reacts with the situation you are in, the role you are playing, and is affected by the culture you are in, and this creates outputs that we call behaviors. Your behavior is nothing more than the words you use (content) with a musical pitch, tone, and volume; facial mask (expressions); eye contact; and body language. We catch all of this and make an assessment as to what you really mean. Our personalities process all of that cognitively and instantaneously, and behave or react back in an exchange of communication, which could be positive or negative or a mix.

Everyone has a personality, but this is hidden; the deep you, what makes you tick, what you believe in, and your values are mostly hidden from us. But as soon as you open your mouth, make some eye contact, use facial expressions, and your body language, I can access your world, I can see what makes you tick and start to uncover what defines you as a person. I can see your level of introversion or extroversion; I can hear the pitch, tone, and volume of your voice; and I can observe your body language and how open or closed it is. I can tune into your words and pick out the key ones and truly start to listen not just hear what you are saying and what is behind all this. Moreover, I can now use colors not so many words to describe it and the color should reflect the behavior being used.

Think of red—what comes to mind for you? I hope you will see passion and drive, risk taking, competitive with high energy, fire in their belly, an aggression in them, or at least an ability to be assertive.

Think of yellow—bright, sunny, positive, happy, social, and outgoing.

Think of blue—cold, cool, calculating, logical, clam, practical, and unemotional.

Think of green—ecological, growing ideas and growing relationships, earthy, and emotional—high emotional Intelligence (EQ—the ability to recognize your own and others' emotions and tune into them)—(Daniel Goleman).

As we go through the book I want you to be focused on why you are reading this book—to understand yourself like you have never understood yourself before and to understand others too. What makes you and them tick? What causes the clashes between the inner you and other people?—between two teams and two cultures, maybe even within your organization? Do you have two departments, where cross team working is vital, but is also the biggest issue facing your businesses. I have seen this in almost every organization.

Marketing—we can invent anything you can dream of.

Sales—we can sell this to you and you can have it tomorrow.

Operations—what !!!!!!? We can't do that for months! We are already too busy.

Purchasing—we have not even ordered the bits to make it yet because no one told us you wanted it.

Invoicing—the customer is complaining that we have invoiced for a product they have not yet received—what is going on?

Customer Services—we are getting low scores from our client satisfaction surveys and so there is a problem.

Training team in human resources (HR)—all the staff need training in Customer services.

Directors—we are not making any money and yet you are spending what we haven't got on training.

Personnel team in HR—I think we need to make some redundancies.

HR—now staff morale is on the floor, we need to do some well-being and coaching with the team leaders.

And so on …

In the construction industry in the United Kingdom, there is a standard process that is not dissimilar to this.

1. Bid for work at zero profit so we can win the project. Put together without consultation of the actual people who should build it, using estimators (guesswork) and other pre-construction staff, most of whom have never set foot on a building site.

2. Win project with end date in six months with no negotiation for an extension of time—client (end user) must take occupation on a certain date.

3. In the interim we are flat out with all staff fully engaged on other projects.

4. No proper project launch with site managers, project managers, subcontractors, surveyors, buyers, client, end users in this meeting about three months before the multi-million-pound job starts.

5. Go live day—delayed by three weeks as we have no staff.

6. Token gesture made—hoardings put up three weeks late.

7. Site manager goes to job having never even seen the drawings and starts ordering materials. The surveyor selects cheapest subcontractors, who are also busy and cannot start as per original time plan.

8. Site loses one day a week in slippage through inefficiencies and materials not being available or any number of surprises, like finding hidden asbestos, unexploded Second World War bomb, or ground workers dig through water mains and cut off electricity supply for two weeks.

9. The site manager is not trusted by the surveyors and cannot even buy print cartridges or toilet rolls for the site without three signatures, even though he is responsible and accountable for a multimillion-pound job.

10. Meanwhile, Client is totally unaware as no one has said anything except that it is all going well. So, the client is planning to move in on time and is ordering furniture to be delivered and IT to be installed before completion and handover date.

11. This continues until one week before completion date is due, and then client is told they are going to be three months late in handing over.

12. Both sides seek advice from Lawyers.

13. Everyone is blaming everyone else and suing each other for costs and so a court case is likely to happen.

14. The client will not be using the contractor again.

Almost every job in the construction industry overruns, bursts the budget, and has never been snag free on handover.

As you can see as each team, or business process, takes over, it causes a bottle neck/delay or miscommunication. Some of you may remember the British 4 × 100-meter relay team of Gardener, Devonish, Lewis-Francis, and Campbell, in the 2004 Olympics winning the gold against all the odds. The American team of Crawford, Gatlin, Miller, and Greene were a much stronger team individually. Gatlin had won gold in the 100M individual event already and Greene had won Bronze in the same event. None of the British team even made the final, but because they handed the baton over perfectly between the legs of the team event and the runners had practiced this, and the United States team did not, the USA team stumbled and clumsily handed over the baton and their timing was out. The British Team beat them into 2nd place. They should have been 3–4 seconds faster over 400 meters but were in fact 1 second slower. They lost 5 seconds or over 38–40 second race—more than 10% loss of efficiency.

As they handed their work on to the next person in the team there was an issue, a bottleneck, a clash, and it isn't what they did, it was how they did it.

It isn't usually what you have done, but it is how you did it. People will forgive you if you can't do something well but rarely if you won't do it well. In the United Kingdom, the biggest single issue at work is not competence or capabilities, it is conduct. Much of the employee relations (ER) cases are those in which people have behaved inappropriately not because they did a bad job. We call this the can't do/won't do dilemma. If somebody can't do, you can train them, teach them, and coach them, but if they won't do it, what can you do about it other than taking disciplinary action and issue warnings.

So, the post arrives and person A's job is to open it and circulate it; so methodically and carefully he or she opens it letter by letter and reads them, sorts into piles, and then goes on rounds distributing them, starting at the bottom of the building in room one to room two and so on until he or she gets to the top and last office. So, if carefully and methodically done, tick in box and now move on to next job or task. What if the chief executive officer (CEO) is desperately waiting for a cheque to arrive or an order to arrive that is critical to the business; he wanted and demanded this to be handed to him on its arrival? But he gets it last. He is now angry and the post person is feeling wounded and sulky at doing what he or she thought was a good job. It might be a poor example but I have seen many of these over the years and here are a few.

A Medical Secretary worked from the top of the pile in his or her tray, so the stuff at the bottom was left and in one case there was a life-threatening letter that needed urgent action but was left for weeks as the person never quite got to the bottom.

- Two teams not talking to each other because the team leaders disagree on what and how stuff should move between departments—resulting in deliberate acts to slow down or annoy each other—"infighting."
- An invoice clerk not paying an invoice for months as it was incorrectly dated but had been signed by the CEO to pay and so they took no action, just left it to one side. The unpaid supplier withdrew his or her services for nonpayment.
- A call center sending out a Gas registered fitter to someone's house to fix an electric water heater because they did not ask one extra question and reacted to "My boiler doesn't work!" costing the company $100 in lost time and an unhappy customer.

They all treated the person how they would like to be treated—methodically, or angrily, or carefully and step by step, or too fast. But if all of the parties involved had changed their behavior and treated the other person how THEY wanted to be treated, then the invoice clerk would have acted more urgently, the two team leaders would have been more cooperative and understanding of each other, the Doctor's letter would have been dealt with quickly with urgency and speed, and the call center would have been more thorough in the investigative stage and truly understood the issues. We misunderstand others' facial expressions, body language, and voice pitch and volume all the time.

What causes this to happen? Well, according to a Harvard Business school study and using psychologists from American Psychological

Society (APS) and British Psychological Society (BPS), as experts, they came up with a simple explanation in a paper published in 2014 entitled "Behaviors—why do we behave the way we do?" and in simple terms it said this: There are two main reasons why we behave inappropriately. The first is we have forgotten how to use our behaviors effectively and they have become so slight we cannot differentiate between two similar expressions anymore and the second is that even if someone does use good behavioral signals we are not even looking, listening, or paying attention, and would rather look at our mobile phones, laptops, tablets, the TV, or some other distraction—they called these the transparency illusion and the cognitive miser.

1. The Transparency Illusion states that our facial expressions can be so similar that others misunderstand them—the difference between being puzzled, concerned, nervous, and angry might be so similar in some people that we react incorrectly to it.
2. The Cognitive Miser says we are not even looking properly, not paying enough attention to another person or team, are so focused on ourselves, we glance and do not look at what is behind the facial mask/expression, are more interested in the need to win or be above the next person, and this can be increased by the proximity we have to another person, both physical and the relationship creating relative jealousy.

I have always called this your "sensing mechanism" an imaginary sensor we all have, which is looking ahead, like your own personal radar looking around to see if there is any change. So when you walk into a room, your sensing mechanism knows something bad has happened, or that danger is close by or in some people there is a lack of this awareness or sensitivity to a situation. Humans have this instinct to be able to quickly sense a situation they are in as dangerous, funny, risky, serious, or worrying, without being told to laugh or cry or run away. Prehistoric man could sense these threats from miles away as could most animals; look at a Giraffe or a Zebra when a pride of lions approaches and see what they do when an attack is likely; they flock together, or run away, or even fight, but the ones who carry on grazing or playing or doing nothing are at greater risk of being caught. We have lost this ability or at least it has become atrophied or dormant. We fall down holes, walk into beams, or say or do the wrong thing at the wrong time without always sensing what is required. You don't treat others as you want to be treated, but instead treat others as they want to be treated, a 180-degree paradigm shift from what we are taught as children. The human ego is what we are talking about: distortion and bias. We can distort what we see, hear, and sense, and we have inbuilt biases too, always favoring one side or another of any decision, situation, and people we are dealing with, more forgiving to one and less to another. This is increased by the closeness and relevance we have to another person. This explains why we might have sibling rivalry and yet second cousin twice removed or a work colleague tends to be less so.

Cristiano Ronaldo and David Beckham, when they both played for Real Madrid, had high relevance (same team, same focus, same objectives, etc.) but lower closeness apart from work, they never sat next to each other or socialized outside of work, whereas David and Victoria Beckham have high closeness (same family, love each other, etc.) but a low relevance to each other at work where there is nearly no overlap apart from charity work. However, Venus and Serena Williams have both closeness and relevance, live and work together, have same family and same sport, and even play against each other and with each other. But Victoria Beckham and Serena Williams have both low closeness and low relevance. So, the greatest risk of rivalry and potential for inappropriate behavior will probably be between the sisters and not Victoria and Serena and less likely between David and Christiano.

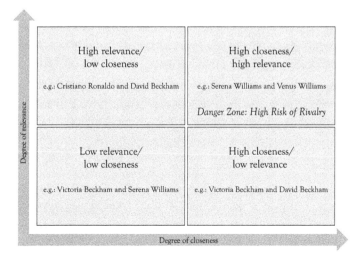

Exercise—Think of you and your partner or best friend and plot them using the aforementioned matrix and then add a work colleague and two others and see if you can see who you are more likely to clash with.

Another way to see how we can misinterpret others' behaviors, and to prove we are poor judges of what we see and hear is in fact that we make most things up based on little evidence or facts. And we do ask more questions before deciding that something is true, and this known as the Fact, Faction, Fiction, Fancy, and Fantasy continuum (by Dr. Gillman—the opium eaters).

Facts—what we know about ourselves; the deep, hidden, and real information that we even hide from our partners; and the only place where near 100 percent fact is true. We know ourselves better than anyone and we know more about ourselves than anyone else.

Faction—what we know about our relatives and loved ones, but not as much as we know about ourselves—75 percent known and 25 percent made up.

Fiction—what we half know and half make up about our work colleagues based on coffee machine communication (what others tell us or we interpret for ourselves often wrongly)—50 percent known and 50 percent made up.

Fancy—Things I want but cannot get and can see that others might have them, creating jealousy or dismissive behaviors—25 percent known and 75 percent made up and nearly all subjective.

Fantasy—what we make up based on our own biases, prejudices, jealousy, and jumping to conclusions based on what we can see and not much else—100 percent made up.

E.G.—I know most about me (Facts) and quite a lot about my wife—but not all! When she is seen by me secretly texting over a few days or weeks I assume that she might be having an affair when in fact she is trying to surprise me for my birthday (Faction). I know even less about my work colleagues and so when I see the accountant come in on a Monday sweating and looking stressed and he goes into his office, shuts the door, and does not say good morning to me, I assume that the company is in some sort of trouble when in fact he has a cold (Fiction). Next (Fancy) you always wanted a Range Rover and your next-door neighbor gets one so you are either jealous of him or dismiss Range Rovers as, everyone's got one, they are gas guzzlers, expensive to run, and people who drive them are tossers. And when my next-door neighbor turns up in another brand new $250,000 (£200,000) car for his wife and she had an old banger for five years, people might assume (fantasy) that he must be a drug dealer or a bank robber. When the fact is that he has inherited money, or had a bonus from work.

Exercise—Think about you and what you know about yourself, think about your partner and what you know about him or her, think about your next-door neighbors and what you know about them, think about a person you see who lives at the end of the street and you always wondered about him or her but don't know much other than that which you can see or someone has told you about him or her. Think of a work colleague who works in a different department and never talked to him or her and what you have assumed about him or her.

We need to get you to be better at understanding yourself better than you did before and more deeply; second, how to understand others; third, how to improve your own ability to judge any situation; and fourth, to use the most appropriate behaviors for that situation and be able to use a wider range of behaviors to become a more influential person, not in weeks or months but in hours or days.

Four Steps

1. Understand yourself, deeper and more than you did before using Spectrum.
2. Understand others better using Spectrum—reading body language, seeing facial expressions, and tuning into another's voice, pitch, volume, and the content—what are they saying.
3. Improve your judgment and ability to read situations intuitively and instinctively.

4. Use the right Behavior or color of the other person—the client—and not stick with your old style or colors (flexing without compromising your beliefs or values).

Try it now, so I can show you how it is possible to influence feelings and behaviors without compromising your values or beliefs. Please make a visible smile for five seconds, now tune into how that made you feel as you simply turned your lips upwards using six facial muscles voluntarily. I bet you felt better, happier even for a few seconds. In call centers, we say: answer the phone with a smile, people can hear a smile down the phone. This is because when you are smiling you are changing the physiology of the roof space in your mouth and this changes how you sound; your lips and cheeks are in a different place so the pitch and tone change and the customer can hear it. It works!

I started using psychometrics (tests to look at behavior and personality) over 30 years ago, and you still need to fill out a form, send it to a Level A or Level B psychologist or an accredited analyst, who then gives you his or her expert opinion in a week's time. This drives us nuts; so we created our own online method, which is instant, easy to understand, and you will be able to use it today, tomorrow, and forever. Even today with online websites it is hard to find free or cheap methods of assessing your behavioral profile and get instant access to the data; the average I believe is £150 ($200) for each one.

Everyone knows the word "behavior," everyone uses it, and yet here we are in the twenty-first century and it is the world's best kept secret; only for use by analysts, doctors, therapists, and counselors, all with qualifications. But we behave 24 hours a day and 365 days a year. We behave well, badly, normally, abnormally, naughtily, sexily, funnily, crossly, sulkily, moodily, wittily, and so on, but with no easy-to-use method of improvement or feedback. But what does that mean? What is it? Ask anyone what behavior is and you get a thousand answers, all different and without a clear easy-to-understand definition or explanation of what it is. As children, we are told by our parents "Behave yourself." What does that mean? It means "don't embarrass me!" Also as children we inherit approximately 50 percent of our personality from our mothers and her ancestors and 50 percent from our father's lineage, therefore, 50 percent of their behaviors too; we then spend the next 15 years copying our role models, and then get told off when they see us behaving like them. Freud said, "Show me the father and I will show you the son!" He was half right.

It is simple, it is not so much what you do, it is how you do it. It is the correct use of your face, with matching eyes and body language and with words in an appropriate pitch, tone, and volume so that we get our message across and they judge us on this. Then we hear back from the other party, and can see their face and eyes, hear their words, and then judge them as behavior. A managing director is a brilliant, inspirational leader, but when he presents he falls to pieces with nerves. Technically brilliant, we are receiving his facial mask and eyes as terror, his shaking legs and hands as fear, his trembling voice as someone who has no confidence, and decide not to buy from him. If he could learn to turn the nerves into confidence, disguise the terror as energy, and hide the shaking legs and hands by changing his behavior suddenly, he seems less nervous. Now he walks around the stage so that the legs cannot be seen shaking, and he puts his notes away that were accentuating his trembling hands. He uses red and yellow behaviors to give his 5-minute talk and so raises his voice volume, pitch, and tone, and maybe adds a joke or two and a different animal is being seen by the customers now. His values have not changed and his beliefs have not moved. He is still the same man and guess what, the next time he is asked to present, he will feel more confident than last time.

We all have a personality that is partly inherited from our parents and then the rest is learned and copied as we go into adulthood from babies (Nature and Nurture)—this leads us to having thoughts that lead to emotions and then feelings, which come out as an output called behavior. How do we react to situations, the roles we play, the relationships we have, the cultures we live in, and the environment around us.

Here we attempt to give you a simple way to describe behavior and to look at your own and others' behaviors, both clearly understanding yourself and others using colors not words and be able to influence them positively, so that you get the outcome you are looking for, using colors that relate to behaviors that are easily remembered and for "normal" everyday situations where we are relaxed, when we are stressed out, and how we change under pressure or not. There are four levels of stress: 1—normal; 2—positive stress where we have heightened reactions and can go higher, further, faster, and have very high performance; 3—negative stress where we overuse our behaviors, our performance dips, and we are seen as struggling; and of course 4—distress—where we cannot cope and hide away, become depressed, be uncommunicative, and be unable to cope with "normal" life situations—here is where heavy drinking, substance abuse, and violence as well as depression can be seen.

1. Normal behaviors every day use auto pilot.
2. Positive stress at work under slight pressure performing to your best for short periods—a presentation to a client, winning a contract, an interview or in sport taking a penalty/kicking a field goal, making a tackle, and so on.
3. Negative stress—using too much of any one behavior, excessive behaviors, struggling to perform, getting cross, sulking, uncommunicative, silly, ignoring serious stuff, avoiding doing important and urgent stuff and focusing on the trivia, hiding, and in sport late tackle, giving a foul away, missing a penalty or field goal, and so on.
4. Distress—cannot cope—fight, flight, freeze, frolic, or flock, unacceptable vocal and physical actions at work or at home or in sport—red card; running away, taking time off with stress, avoiding work, seeking medical help, taking drugs, smoking or excessive drinking, doing nothing at all, inaction, hiding in meetings but contributing zero; messing about with stuff that has no effect on the business, restructuring for no purpose, team building when team is okay, changing the brand for the sake of changing the brand, and focusing on values when everything seems okay.

Exercise—describe situations that you have been in, in each of the four aforementioned behaviors and find at least one that fills you with dread and that you avoid and potentially makes you feel like you cannot cope.

I would say that 90 percent of what I have been asked to help companies with is negative staff, stress, poor performance, and lack of motivation that individuals and teams suffer at work. It is either one person who needs help, or a team, or an organization that is in a negative stress or distressful situation. Eighty percent of what you do at work is directly attributed to behaviors—how you do your tasks and only 20 percent to technical skills and knowledge. And yet organizations spend 80 percent of their training budget on the technical stuff, which is madness. If a training intervention made a 10 percent difference to the performance of staff and you focus the training on technical stuff, you will only improve things by 2 percent (10 percent of the 20 percent). But if you spend the same amount on soft skills and behaviors, leadership and management/supervisory skills, and it has the same impact, you will make 8 percent difference (10 percent of the 80 percent). And when companies are under pressure what do they slash? It is the training budget, thinking it is saving them money. We have measured the effectiveness of training in several organizations where we have focused on soft skills and behaviors and the result was: approximately for every £1 spent £10 back from performance improvements in staff, efficiencies and higher motivation, effective leadership and happier teams.

We usually get called in when the boss of a company says—the turnover is down, profits are down, we cannot win work, this team is a poor performing team/department, this individual is a poor performing individual (usually one of the senior managers), the staff do not live the values, the morale is falling, staff or customer satisfaction is falling, massive changes are occurring in the local or global marketplace.

But, rarely, the product is poor. This led me to believe that it is not **what** we make or provide but **how** we do it that is the issue. I have been a soft skills trainer, that is, behavior, coaching, and counseling individuals and working as a management consultant; training, learning, and development specialist; employee relations expert, mediator, and facilitator as well as an "expert" in Human Resources for over 30 years and am qualified in Organizational Psychology, Life Coaching, CBT counseling, and Psychometrics. I discovered that all the behavioral models are good, but expensive to use, difficult to remember the next day, unusable, need interpreting by an "expert" who must be "qualified" in that model, and it can take days before you get any feedback and then who walks away leaving you interested and turned on by the new concept, but confused and unable to move any further forward without more costly help and with the "so what" factor!

So let us now do a full color profile using SPECTRUM online if you can—and get a report that you can print out and read, only $14.99 and £9.99 for yourself, then you can use this as we go through the book and this will help you move forward, to persuade others, negotiate situations, sell more, and just get others to be more on your wavelength after just an hour or so of using it. Here you can also find other surveys on team effectiveness, strategy, learning and teaching styles, teamwork, and many more: www.evaluationstore.com. Please complete yours as quickly and honestly as you can.

If you e-mail evaluationstore.com on their website, they will provide you with a 50% discount code 7; all you have to provide is your e-mail address and quote the book title "Across the Spectrum" by Stephen Elkins-Jarrett.

CHAPTER 5

Creating Your Own Profile—Online or Paper Based

If you can go online and complete a profile it is a more detailed profile with normal and stress and ABC included and Has a Lot More Information for You—However, If You Prefer a Free Paper-Based Version Then you can Use This One—if you e-mail www.evaluationstore.com they will issue you a 50% off code by mentioning that name of this book and the author. Please place a cross or dot on the score for each and every answer you give.

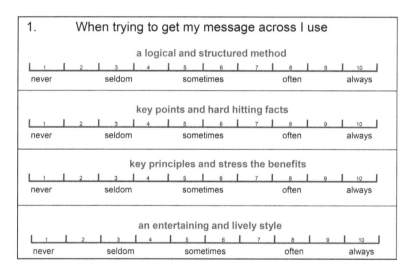

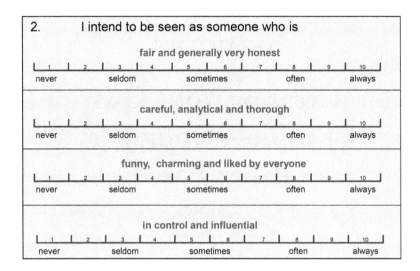

2.   I intend to be seen as someone who is

fair and generally very honest

| 1 | 2 | 3 | 4 | 5 | 6 | 7 | 8 | 9 | 10 |
| never | | seldom | | sometimes | | | often | | always |

careful, analytical and thorough

| 1 | 2 | 3 | 4 | 5 | 6 | 7 | 8 | 9 | 10 |
| never | | seldom | | sometimes | | | often | | always |

funny, charming and liked by everyone

| 1 | 2 | 3 | 4 | 5 | 6 | 7 | 8 | 9 | 10 |
| never | | seldom | | sometimes | | | often | | always |

in control and influential

| 1 | 2 | 3 | 4 | 5 | 6 | 7 | 8 | 9 | 10 |
| never | | seldom | | sometimes | | | often | | always |

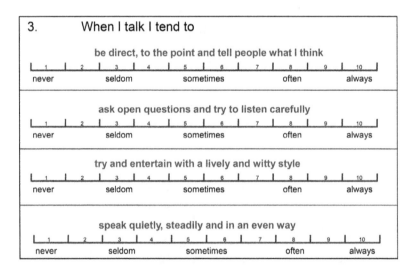

3.   When I talk I tend to

be direct, to the point and tell people what I think

| 1 | 2 | 3 | 4 | 5 | 6 | 7 | 8 | 9 | 10 |
| never | | seldom | | sometimes | | | often | | always |

ask open questions and try to listen carefully

| 1 | 2 | 3 | 4 | 5 | 6 | 7 | 8 | 9 | 10 |
| never | | seldom | | sometimes | | | often | | always |

try and entertain with a lively and witty style

| 1 | 2 | 3 | 4 | 5 | 6 | 7 | 8 | 9 | 10 |
| never | | seldom | | sometimes | | | often | | always |

speak quietly, steadily and in an even way

| 1 | 2 | 3 | 4 | 5 | 6 | 7 | 8 | 9 | 10 |
| never | | seldom | | sometimes | | | often | | always |

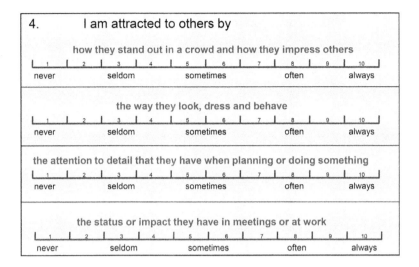

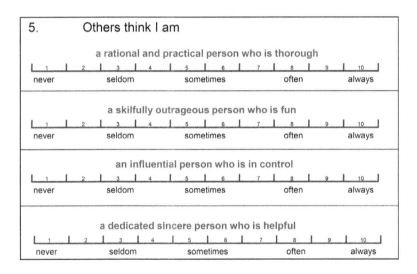

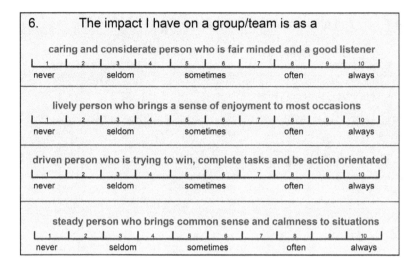

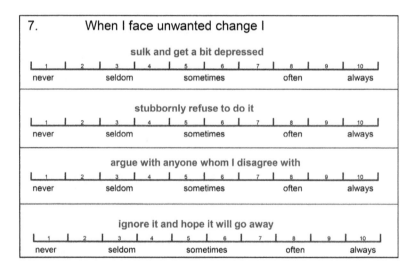

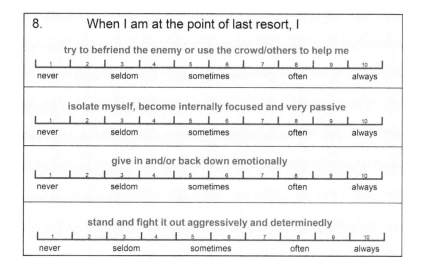

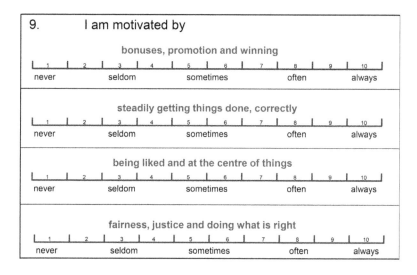

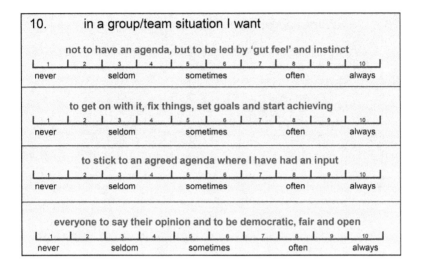

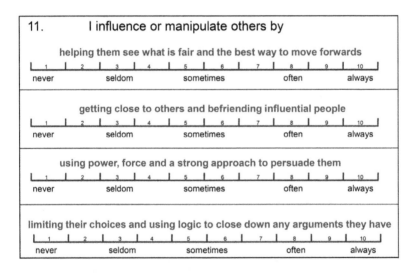

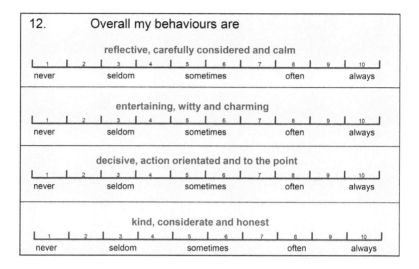

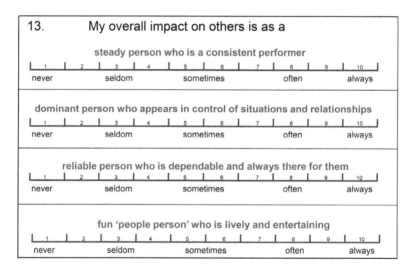

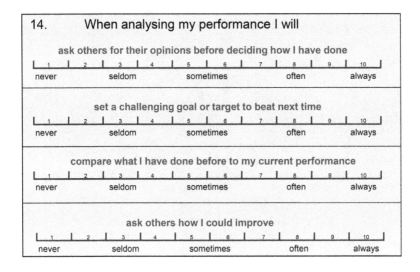

14.   When analysing my performance I will

ask others for their opinions before deciding how I have done

| 1 | 2 | 3 | 4 | 5 | 6 | 7 | 8 | 9 | 10 |

never   seldom   sometimes   often   always

set a challenging goal or target to beat next time

| 1 | 2 | 3 | 4 | 5 | 6 | 7 | 8 | 9 | 10 |

never   seldom   sometimes   often   always

compare what I have done before to my current performance

| 1 | 2 | 3 | 4 | 5 | 6 | 7 | 8 | 9 | 10 |

never   seldom   sometimes   often   always

ask others how I could improve

| 1 | 2 | 3 | 4 | 5 | 6 | 7 | 8 | 9 | 10 |

never   seldom   sometimes   often   always

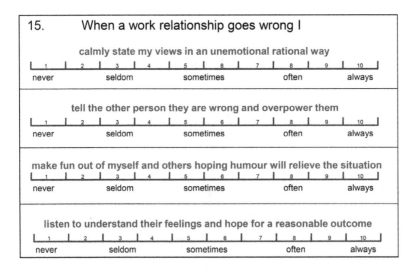

15.   When a work relationship goes wrong I

calmly state my views in an unemotional rational way

| 1 | 2 | 3 | 4 | 5 | 6 | 7 | 8 | 9 | 10 |

never   seldom   sometimes   often   always

tell the other person they are wrong and overpower them

| 1 | 2 | 3 | 4 | 5 | 6 | 7 | 8 | 9 | 10 |

never   seldom   sometimes   often   always

make fun out of myself and others hoping humour will relieve the situation

| 1 | 2 | 3 | 4 | 5 | 6 | 7 | 8 | 9 | 10 |

never   seldom   sometimes   often   always

listen to understand their feelings and hope for a reasonable outcome

| 1 | 2 | 3 | 4 | 5 | 6 | 7 | 8 | 9 | 10 |

never   seldom   sometimes   often   always

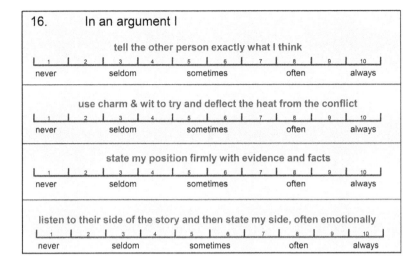

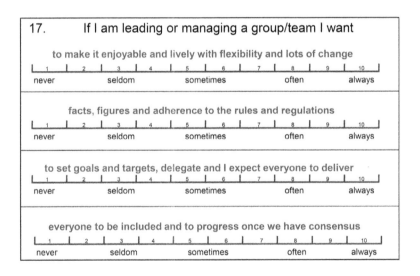

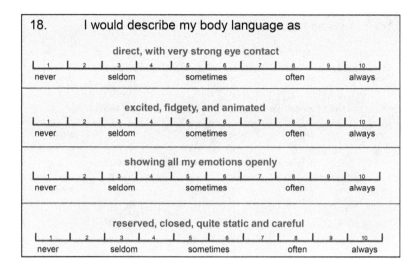

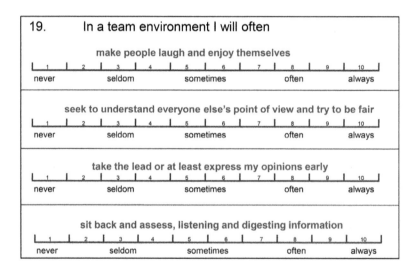

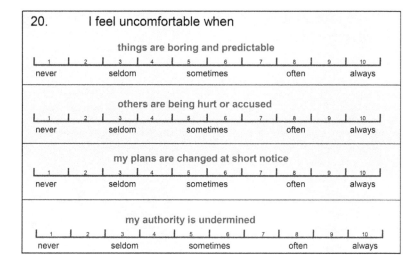

20.   I feel uncomfortable when

things are boring and predictable

| 1 | 2 | 3 | 4 | 5 | 6 | 7 | 8 | 9 | 10 |
never   seldom   sometimes   often   always

others are being hurt or accused

| 1 | 2 | 3 | 4 | 5 | 6 | 7 | 8 | 9 | 10 |
never   seldom   sometimes   often   always

my plans are changed at short notice

| 1 | 2 | 3 | 4 | 5 | 6 | 7 | 8 | 9 | 10 |
never   seldom   sometimes   often   always

my authority is undermined

| 1 | 2 | 3 | 4 | 5 | 6 | 7 | 8 | 9 | 10 |
never   seldom   sometimes   often   always

Be careful to put your scores in the right box—place your answers from top to bottom on each question not left to right.

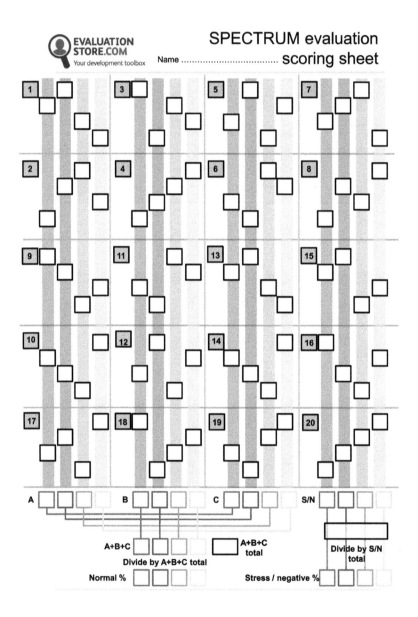

CHAPTER 6

Introduction to the Four Primary Colors

This chapter introduces you to the four basic colors. At least 4,000 years ago, people started studying behaviors. After the Second World War, psychologist started focusing on modeling and analysis of behaviors. All the current models were created or adapted from 1940, 50s, and 60s right through today. I believe there are over 250 of these in use currently and I cannot see any differences among them. So what is new and different about SPECTRUM?

It is simplified and easier to use than any of the other behavioral models by creating a new one based on four primary colors or behaviors just like all the other models but for the first time; and as far as we know, added blends of two, three, and four colors of behaviors, which create for the first time additional, secondary, tertiary, and tonal colors, are both memorable and reflect the style that the color represents. So once you think of a color it should reflect the behaviors that the color suggests. This seemed logical to us as very few people use the one behavior that most of the other models have as your first or top behavior, and many are too complicated to remember the next day.

Most questions give you the option to choose one answer—pick one option from the choices, but SPECTRUM lets you choose all four if you want to and allows you to choose from 1 to 10 how much or how strongly you use that behavior. We believe for the first time it truly reflects your opinion of how you behave in any given situation.

Example of old-style questionnaires:

When frustrated with another person at work do you

1. Get cross?
2. Become stubborn?
3. Laugh it off?
4. Sulk and become moody?

And you can only pick ONE.

For the same question, SPECTRUM allows you to choose the following:

By what degree do you

	Never–Seldom–Rarely–Sometimes–Often–Always
Get cross	0 - 1 - 2 - 3 - 4 - 5 - 6 - 7 - 8 - 9 - 10
Become stubborn	0 - 1 - 2 - 3 - 4 - 5 - 6 - 7 - 8 - 9 - 10
Laugh it off	0 - 1 - 2 - 3 - 4 - 5 - 6 - 7 - 8 - 9 - 10
Sulk and become moody	0 - 1 - 2 - 3 - 4 - 5 - 6 - 7 - 8 - 9 - 10

And for every single score, for example, a 2 will equal and slightly change your overall profile, whereas with existing models it is all or nothing in that one answer influences the final outcome.

Spectrum has put their survey online and you get the feedback immediately, not next week when a consultant has to visit you to explain it to you and charge you a large sum of money for doing it. Some of the surveys are even free. Most charge around £150 each compared to the average, which is £150, and is saved for the exclusive use of executives for whom large companies invest for their personal development and the rest of us are ignored. You can even use this same website to analyze a team, company, a department, and so on. It can also be used to look at another person, a client, or a customer so that you will find it easier to sell to them. A partner, a son or daughter, a boss and member of staff, or even when recruiting someone, the list is endless.

So now let me introduce you to the four basic, prime colors or styles. If you now compare our simple method to all these quite complicated, expensive, and difficult-to-interpret models, where you might need an expert to interpret the data, you will see how easy it is and that you are already an expert.

Let me now introduce you to SPECTRUM: Specific, Personal, Effective, Communication, Through Really Understanding Me.

You answer a few questions online, honestly and we give you the main, most important values and the behaviors that you feel most at home with the areas of underuse, overuse, and potential early warning signals, which can help you to change color and be more effective at everything you do. What about the cut-down version first? It is that simple to get a flavor in one or two questions but after 20 the real you comes out. How introvert or extrovert do you see yourself as: extremely introvert, quite introvert, neither introvert nor extrovert, quite extrovert, and finally extremely extrovert. Give this a score, where 0 is totally introvert and 10 is totally extrovert.

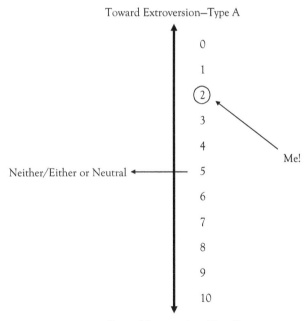

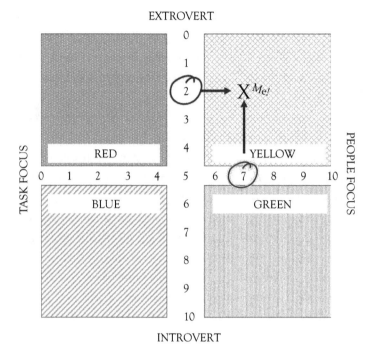

Next ask yourself how people or task focused are you? Here 0 is totally task focused and people just get in the way; 5 is both people and task focused; and 10 is totally people focused and tasks just get in the way of relationships and people—it is all about people. Then join the two lines. The midway point could be your color and after just two questions. After just two questions I have a base color or primary color. My color is yellow.

Task focused	Very	Quite	Slightly	Either both	Slightly	Quite	Very	People focused
0–1	1	2	3	4–5	6	7	8	9–10

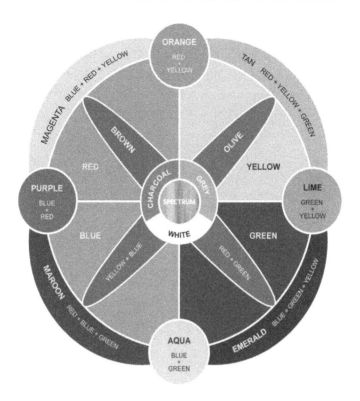

CHAPTER 7

Introduction to All 18 Colors—Overview

There are four primary colors: Red, blue, green, and yellow. This chapter discusses mixing the colors, and blending the behaviors into 18 colors.

Think of **red**—what does this conjure up for you?: Fire, blood, heat, danger. Well that is it, these are the red behaviors; substitute these words for assertive, risk taking, hot headed, combustion, and anger, and you have it. Eureka!

Think of **blue** and you should be thinking cold, water, sky, icebergs; substitute these words for calculating, calm, unemotional, thinking logically, and safety.

Think of **green** and you might start seeing grass, trees, ecologically friendly, peace; and again substitute these words for friendly, growing relationships, fairness, justice, and you have green behavior.

Last, imagine **yellow** and you will see the sun, brightness, and maybe gold; well substitute these words for positive, smiley, warm, and happy and so you now have the whole model—well just about, there are a few things we need to add.

As we add more questions to the profile we start to plot new places across the map, thus creating a four-sided shape and in the full report you have answered 20 questions.

Twin Blends—Secondary Colors

So, what if you have two colors that you see at the same time? Well then we mix those two colors together to create new colors (please remember that these are metaphors for behavior and some of the names of the colors may not truly reflect the actual color you might get if you actually mixed these two colors together).

Blue and red give purple—a task-focused person

Yellow and red give orange—very extrovert, lively, and entertaining

Green and blue give aqua—everything in its place and a place for everything and introvert

Green and yellow give lime—people focused

Yellow and blue give olive—with a dry sense of humor, getting things done right and that will be liked by others

Lastly, red and green give brown—fast paced but seeking high quality, a serious task master, getting results and winning the right way, fairly but can be quite a tough practical person.

Tertiary Colors

Some people might have three colors being equally used. So we have four triple blends, as follows:

Red, blue, and green—called maroon: more introvert than extrovert but a quality-driven perfectionist having a hard side, someone who does not like to be let down, a task-driven person.

Yellow, blue, and green—called emerald: more introvert but with a sense of humor, which is hidden, but can be quietly outrageous. Detail is important but being liked is also important, more people oriented than task, quietly outrageous, perfectionists.

Blue, red, and yellow—called Magenta: task focused but with a fun side, creative problem solver, likes being in teams and innovative.

Red, yellow, and green—called tan: more extrovert than introvert but driven by being liked, doing things well and having a confidence in their own ability, slightly more extrovert than introvert, driven to achieve, and a great confidence in one's own ability. Focused on the shorter/medium term.

Tonal Colors

And, of course, there is a small number of people, who have flat, level, or equal scores of all four colors—and these can be all low, all medium, or all high scores, and so we define these using the **white**–grey scale. From white for low scores, grey for medium, charcoal for medium high, and finally SPECTRUM for very high.

White would be a quite flat, serious, and possibly even a bit dull and use low levels of behaviors (small movements, quiet voice, low eye contact, and straight faced). It would appear deep and might require some coaching and help. Quiet, a low risk tasker and low levels of apparent confidence, possibly low self-esteem.

Grey would be a slightly higher user of the behaviors but still deep and serious, but very quiet. Introvert, calm, slow, deliberate, a steady eddy, predictable performer, WYSIWYG (what you see is what you get).

Charcoal would be a good user of all behaviors and appears to be close to something great, but often falling short and slightly missing the opportunity to excel—more extrovert, confident, and all rounder; uses all behaviors equally; is a good performer; and is usually career and status motivated.

SPECTRUM is the pinnacle of all behaviors, or is it? Someone who is in total control and always uses the right behavior at the right time with the right person to get what they want, but maybe just their own opinion. Egotistical? To be truly inspirational, I believe others must also see the same qualities in you, as you see in yourself. They are high performers, have high self-esteem, are inspirational leaders, and are excellent at what they do. They are wise, always use the right behavior, at the right time, in the right way, so that they get a win/win for all. Do you know anyone like this?

However, please be careful with any color that you do not label yourself with forever as your profile can change with time. Others may see you differently, and you may change at home, at work, and in your social groups. Keep being aware of the nuances of the facial expressions, keep tuned in to their body language, or if you are struggling to do it intuitively, then it is always worth getting them to fill out a report on you or better still complete a 360-degree survey, where many others can comment on you. These are both available at www.evaluationstore.com. These can be more powerful than your view of yourself. Remember it is how you come across to others that matters.

And let us summarize what behavior is one last time and to make it more understandable using the "two-year-old test." In the film *Phila- delphia*, Tom Hanks, who plays a top lawyer, and one who has acquired immunodeficiency syndrome (AIDS), is trying to sue his employer for unfair dismissal and discrimination, but no one takes the case, until he goes further and further down the food chain of lawyers until he finds Denzel Washington, a small claims injury lawyer, the lowest of low in America. But when Tom Hanks starts giving Denzel a high-level and deeply legal argument, Denzel Washington stops him and says some- thing along the lines of, "explain it to me, like I am a two-year-old child, then everyone will understand it!" Behavior is how we communicate to others—talking, listening, body language, face, and eyes. Remember we have two eyes, two ears, and one mouth, and we should use them in that proportion, twice as much looking, and twice as much listening as talking.

ONE MOUTH
So one word spoken to two heard and seen

TWO EYES
So twice as much looking as talking

TWO EARS
So twice as much listening as talking

We can look at, listen, and assess another person without the pro- filing tool. We can look at a group or team; your leadership style; your management and supervisory skills; and your ability to present, persuade, negotiate, sell, or influence another person or group. It can highlight your strengths and your weaknesses. How to minimize the weaknesses and maximize the strengths. This is a simple diagnostic and not scientific but surprisingly accurate. This is very good for quickly seeing that I am more yellow and you are more red and that we need to treat each other as WE WANT TO BE TREATED. Each person has a focus that we should try to mirror or match or deliver. Be careful when mirroring red. It is better to deliver what they want rather than match their behaviors. Each color heads toward the following.

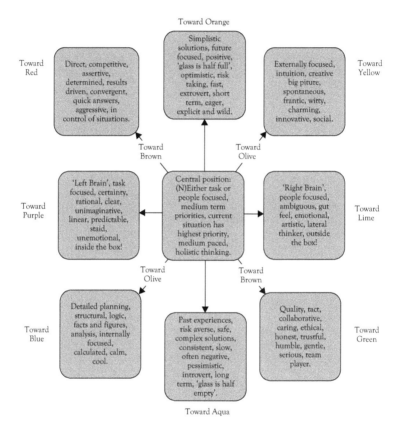

Toward Orange

Toward Red

Direct, competitive, assertive, determined, results driven, convergent, quick answers, aggressive, in control of situations.

Simplistic solutions, future focused, positive, 'glass is half full', optimistic, risk taking, fast, extrovert, short term, eager, explicit and wild.

Externally focused, intuition, creative big piture, spontaneous, frantic, witty, charming, innovative, social.

Toward Yellow

Toward Brown

Toward Olive

Toward Purple

'Left Brain', task focused, certainty, rational, clear, unimaginative, linear, predictable, staid, unemotional, inside the box!

Central position: (N)Either task or people focused, medium term priorities, current situation has highest priority, medium paced, holistic thinking.

'Right Brain', people focused, ambiguous, gut feel, emotional, artistic, lateral thinker, outside the box!

Toward Lime

Toward Olive

Toward Brown

Toward Blue

Detailed planning, structural, logic, facts and figures, analysis, internally focused, calculated, calm, cool.

Past experiences, risk averse, safe, complex solutions, consistent, slow, often negative, pessimistic, introvert, long term, 'glass is half empty'.

Quality, tact, collaborative, caring, ethical, honest, trustful, humble, gentle, serious, team player.

Toward Green

Toward Aqua

The whole model

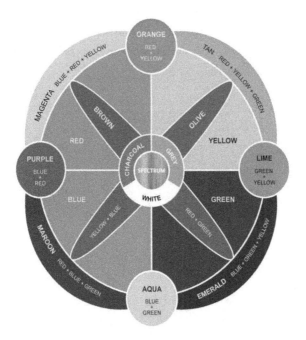

CHAPTER 8

What Does Each Color Mean? Profiles of All 18 Colors—The Detail

In this chapter, we look at the strengths of each color and the early warning signals to excess, the excessive behaviors you might use if under stress, but also underuse—so if a particular color is your lowest percentage score you can also analyze it here. Now you have two color profiles—first is your normal or positive stress color and the second is your negative or stress color—we have not included distress. Look at your two colors, analyze them using the relevant pages, and remember to look at your lowest score and see what that means too.

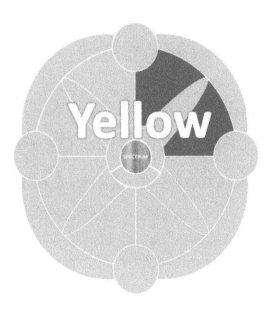

If your highest percentage score is yellow or you came out yellow in your online test then you are likely to be a fun, outgoing person who likes company and social activities; you will be liked and need to be at the center of things, involved and enjoying it.

Yellow people tend to be extroverts, entertaining, funny, witty, charming, and popular. They like to live their lives in the fast lane, enjoying social events and being with people. Teamwork is very important to them. Typically, they enjoy gadgets, new technology, and the latest fashion or trends. They are usually flexible, experimental, and tactful and like to make decisions on what will be liked by others.

Yellow behavior is flexible, experimental, entertaining, sociable, and tactful, and I make decisions on what will be liked by others the most.

Under pressure, you may exhibit frolic or flight-type behavior if pushed.

If this color is your lowest score then you might show these behaviors	If this is your highest score you might be	Early Warning Signal you sometimes come across as	Under Pressure you may even show the following behavior
Rigid	Adaptable	Pliable	Goes with the flow
Unshifting	Exploratory	Speculative	Conjectural
Unsociable	Friendly	Talkative	Gossiping
Unaware	In tune with others	Forgoes own feelings	Insincere
Tactless	Diplomatic	Gratifies others	Appeasing
Limited	Versatile	All rounder	Jack of all master of none
Unimaginative	Ingenious	Over-clever	Tricky
Serious	Witty and funny	A comedian	Absurd or silly
Disagreeable	Pleasant	Too nice	Benign
Real/true	Playacting	Masquerading	Pretending/false

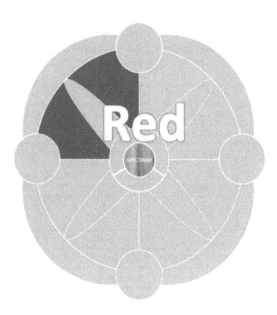

If your highest score is red or your online survey says you are red then you are likely to be a confident person who likes to be in charge of all situations and relationships. You will be decisive and action orientated.

Red people are direct, self-confident, and tend to be extroverts. They tend to use clipped statements and summaries; they are competitive and likely to win everything they do. They want to be successful and will take risks to succeed and achieve. Failure is not an option. Often result driven, fast paced, decisive, persuasive, and with forceful personalities, they welcome change and like to make decisions on what they know. They often act alone and make decisions on impulse. Red behaviors might be competitive, result driven, fast paced, decisive, persuasive, force-ful, welcoming change, and risk taking. Red makes decisions on what he or she knows and usually without others' input; it is his or her decision. They display fight-type behavior if pushed.

If this color is your lowest score then you might show these behaviors	If this is your highest score you might be	Early Warning Signal you sometimes come across as	Under Pressure you may even show the following behavior
Indirect	Straight	Abrupt	Tactless
Slow	Fast reactions	Speedy	Headlong
Humble	Self-assured	Conceited	Egotistical
Conservative	Radical	Draconian	Dictator
Uninspiring	Demanding	Burdensome	Gruelling
Submissive	Dynamic	Domineering	Bullish
Apathetic	Ambitious	Contentious	Combative
Safe	Punter	Exposed	Dangerous
Indecisive	Resolute	Forceful	Overbearing
Mild	Intense	Acute	Agitated

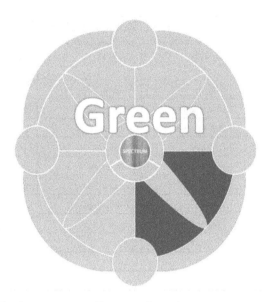

If your highest score was Green or the online report says you are green then you are likely to be a person who strives for excellence and quality and helping others. You will be someone who has a small number of very close and intimate friends whom you trust implicitly.

Green people are passionate about everything. They believe in justice and they care about others and will stop at nothing to get justice. They are usually introverts, honest, trustworthy, and reliable. They like everything to be done to a very high standard; they are sticklers on quality both in materialistic possessions and how work is done.

They tend to be caring, ethical, honest, conscientious, and help-ful, and usually make decisions on emotions, gut feel, and intuition, or instinct. They display lock or fight-type behavior if pushed.

If this color is your lowest score then you might show these behaviors	If this is your highest score you might be	Early Warning Signal you sometimes come across as	Under Pressure you may even show the following behavior
Thoughtless	Attentive	Giving	Charitable
Defeatist	Visionary	Romantic	Dreamer
Confident	Humble	Guilty complex	Self-conscious
Cynical	Naïve	Easily taken in	Unsuspecting
Treacherous	Faithful	Steadfast	Servile
Useless	Obliging	Kind hearted	Soft
Irresponsible	Accountable	Answerable	Takes all the blame
Apathetic	Reactive	Jumps to requests	Anxious and nervy
Flawed	Exemplary	Impeccable	Precise and exacting
Neutral	Critical	Judgmental	Scathing
Conscious	Intuitive	Knee-jerk reaction	Emotional

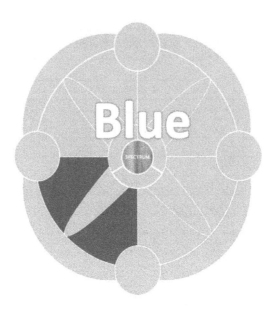

If your highest score was blue then you are likely to be a careful person, who likes to get things right first time, without mistakes. A planner, who needs to know what the result should look like, so that you can achieve this without any surprises at all.

Blue people are careful and like to do things right first time. Usually introverts, they are methodical; risk averse; enjoy structures, rules, and regulations; and make decisions based on facts. They are calm, measured, and reflective. You will never hurry a blue person. They are seen by others as careful, risk averse, sometimes stubborn, definite, rational, calm, structured, and organized. They reflect and think deeply before making any decisions.

Blue behaviors might be careful, risk averse, stubborn, definite, rational, calm, structured, and organized, and blue makes decisions on facts and figures only. Freeze-type behavior is displayed if pushed.

If this color is your lowest score then you might show these behaviors	If this is your highest score you might be	Early Warning Signal you sometimes come across as	Under Pressure you may even show the following behavior
Weak	Unshakable	Resolute	Obstinate
Idealistic	Pragmatic	Empirical	Scientific
Careless	Cautious	Too safe	Pedestrian
Outgoing	Reticent	Restrained	Private
Biased	Detached	Away from	Uninterested
Unstable	Steady	Immovable	Stationary
Careless	Rigorous	Meticulous	Painstaking
Shallow	Systematic	Critical	Analysis paralysis
Extravagant	Thrifty	Frugal	Tight
Messy	Efficient	Meticulous	Punctilious

But what if I use two behaviors equally? Then we have Twin Blends and the first of these is shown here.

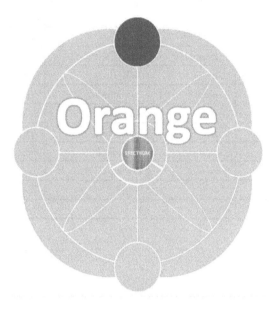

If your scores are very close to each other in red and yellow say less than 1 percent or 2 percent or if the online survey says you are Orange, then you are likely to be an extrovert, very outgoing, lively, and entertaining and at the center of things. Being with people is more important to you than tasks; ad hoc planning and being impulsive, winning, and reacting to demands drive you. You are future focused, quite risk taking, do short-term planning, friendly, and sometimes simplistic in finding solutions.

If you are orange, you will be very extrovert, focused on the outside world and do everything at a very fast pace. You will want to be a winner at everything you do, but you will probably do too much to have enough focus, enjoying the variety of life and the spice of life to the full. You will enjoy others' company and being at the center and controlling events, situations, and relationships trying to keep everyone involved and active. I bet you cannot sit still for more than a few moments and you probably twitch your toes or feet while doing anything. Action, fun, sporty, racy, risky, and lively will be your key words and you will love being the center of attention and you can be outrageous: Frolic, flight, or fight.

If this color is your lowest score then you might show these behaviors	If this is your highest score you might be	Early Warning Signal you sometimes come across as	Under Pressure you may even show the following behavior
Pessimistic	Optimistic	Hopeful	Dreaming
Leisurely	Speedy	Hasty	Whirlwind
Silent	Talkative	Yakking	Rambling
Unsure	Self-confident	Certain	Definite
Boring	Captivating	Seductive	Smarmy
Stubborn	Changeable	Chameleon	Whimsical
Pedantic	Driving	Racing	Breakneck
Apathetic	Enthusiastic	Ebullient	Vehement
Uninterested	Eager	Ardent	Fervent
Planned	Spontaneous	Impulsive	Knee-jerk

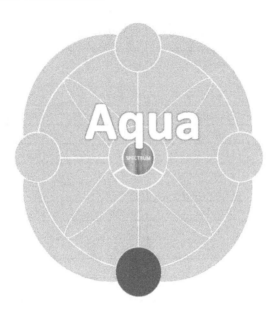

Next, if you come across to others as AQUA or your blue and green scores are within 1 percent or 2 percent then you are likely to be an introvert, probably a quiet person who keeps to himself or herself, producing your best when left to work alone and to use deep, logical, and high-quality thinking to solve your own issues. You like long-term detailed plans and no surprises. You like to use experience and past solutions to find a way forward, and are a long-term planner, who is risk averse, logical, and uses reasoning.

If you are Aqua you are the antipathy of the aforementioned; you will be very introvert, internally focused and a real thinker, proactive, and neat and tidy both in self and thinking. Everything in its place and a place for everything could be your slogan. You will be a quiet, calm, relaxed person who enjoys very nice things and for a long time, you will be focused on achieving something to the end. Long-term projects with a high-quality outcome will be your aim. You prefer small groups of very close friends and family to those large social events where you are a stranger. You will not want to be the center of attention and may even avoid the spotlight and rarely take unmeasured risks—Flock or Freeze.

If this color is your lowest score then you might show these behaviors	If this is your highest score you might be	Early Warning Signal you sometimes come across as	Under Pressure you may even show the following behavior
Active	Passive	Inactive	Dormant
Inconsiderate	Thoughtful	Charitable	Benevolent
Unreliable	Reliable	Devoted	Slavish
Carefree	Anxious	Agitated	Distressed
Outgoing	Reserved	Cold	Withdrawn
Loud	Quiet	Silent	Uncommunicative
Unethical	Ethical	Lawful	Righteous
Light-hearted	Sober	Serious	Solemn
Optimistic	Pessimistic	Negative	Depressed
Risk taker	Risk averse	Safe	Unenterprising

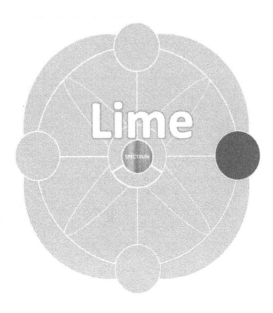

Lime is green and yellow in equal quantities and within 1 percent or 2 percent of each other, and if you have the highest two scores then you are likely to be a people person who likes doing things well and working in teams. Your main drivers will be team performance, collective goals, and group work, so working with others and sharing ideas where quality and innovation are needed.

If you are a Lime, then you are a mixer, a people person, and you will be a mix of introvert and extrovert possibly right in the center. You will have a sense of humor with a skillful ability to mix and be sociable. Again, you will like nice things and new things and possibly the latest gadgets. You will appreciate high-quality things but those that are also noticed and stand out for being of good quality.

Lime People are ambiguous, complex, more right brain than left and use gut feel and intuition to make decisions.

Everything you do has to be done well and has a visual impact, where pictures and fewer words will tell the story. Planning can be long or short if you are motivated and you can react quickly or take your time, based on the reward—Flock, Flight, or Frolic.

If this color is your lowest score then you might show these behaviors	If this is your highest score you might be	Early Warning Signal you sometimes come across as	Under Pressure you may even show the following behavior
Unfriendly	Cordial	Affectionate	Tactile
Intolerant	Tolerant	Forgiving	Lenient
Miserable	Jovial	Lively	Vivacious
Predictable	Innovative	Clever	Egotistical
Uncaring	Caring	Doting	Molly-coddle
Selfish	Selfless	Self-denying	Altruistic
Unkind	Kind	Overgenerous	Obliging
Loner	Collaborative	Fraternize	Conspire
Insensitive	Responsive	Reactive	Jumps to action
Unsociable	Sociable	Chatty	Indulgent

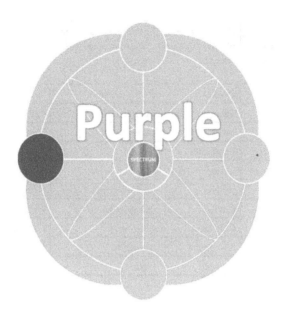

Next is purple, an equal mix of red and blue, where you are likely to be a serious person who is task focused and methodically gets things done one at a time. You will be seen by others as professional, clipped, and unemotional unless irritated. You will speak your mind and not suffer poor performance around you. You expect hard work and output from all.

Purple is the religious color of the Catholic faith and has strong values and morals and so will people who use purple behaviors—not to say they will be religious but will have strong values and morals and expectations of others to be the same. People here are a mix of introvert and extrovert but with an inbuilt quiet confidence, feeling that they know when they are right and they could prove it. It can be seen by others as sinister. Having an inbuilt confidence without having to shout about it, these people get tasks done in a systematic and yet pacy way, on their own and they are usually right.

Sometimes described as a rock showing few emotions, they are predictable and career minded. They will say, without emotion what they need to say, when they need to say it and rarely show any remorse. They will manage rather than lead a team of people and may have casualties along the way, but they will succeed through determination, willpower, knowledge, plans, and goals and objectives—Fight or Freeze.

If this color is your lowest score then you might show these behaviors	If this is your highest score you might be	Early Warning Signal you sometimes come across as	Under Pressure you may even show the following behavior
Inactive	Takes initiative	Dominates	Takes over
Ashamed	Proud	Overjoyed	Gloats
Weak willed	Determined	Relentless	Obstinate
Disorderly	Disciplined	Regimented	Drilled
People focused	Task focused	Mechanistic	Robotic
Dependent	Self-reliant	Independent	Excluding
Indirect	To the point	Frank	Blunt
Gut feel	Evidential	Factual	Proving
Emotional	Rational	Overlogical	Analysis paralysis
Unstructured	Structured	Step by step by step	Dogged

If your main two colors are red and green, then you are Brown, and you are likely to be a serious person who strives for excellence and quality but also tries to do things quickly. You are good at gut feel and using instinct to make decisions, backed up by confidence and a strong set of values.

Brown is usually seen as a natural color and so natural is how other people will describe you; brown people are sticklers on quality and will have a temper if perfection is not reached. They will always fret about speed versus quality and when one wins they will feel that either they could have done it more quickly or better.

They need to have nice things and people around them but having both means they often feel that they are putting more into a relationship than the other party. They spend their lives seeking to help others in a quietly confident way, always approachable, and will surprise others when they throw a tantrum or sulk without any warning—Fight or Flock.

If this color is your lowest score then you might show these behaviors	If this is your highest score you might be	Early Warning Signal you sometimes come across as	Under Pressure you may even show the following behavior
Soft	Hard	Tough	Aggressive
Funny	Serious	Solemn	Sombre
loser	Competitive	Contentious	Combative
Indecisive	Decision maker	Instructing	Forceful
Soft	Disciplinarian	Task master	Tyrant
Lethargic	Vigorous	Energetic	Fiery
Untrusting	Trusting	Loyal	Subservient
Dishonest	Honest	Moralistic	Judgemental
Resistant	Receptive	Open minded	Pliable
Unfaithful	Faithful	Dutiful	Obedient

Next is Olive, an equal mix of yellow and blue. You are likely to be systematic and yet flexible, with a sense of irony and the sardonic. Predictable and innovative, stable and yet adaptable, consistent, and liked by many as a steady performer but with a glint in the eye for being slightly wild, wicked, and naughty.

The Olive is a powerful healthy fruit and can be green or black and you can be both green and black too, you may have a dark side. If you are an olive you will have a very dry and sarcastic or even sardonic sense of humor, quietly dropping the odd comment, which makes most people laugh but usually at the expense of the person you are trying to get at. Others will always know when you are upset or cross with them.

You can be skillfully outrageous. You have the ability to be innovative and creative in your thinking and you will be able to look at things in a new way, while the overwhelming need to do things thoroughly will keep you focused on the long-term objectives.

The frustration might be caused by your need to change while staying the same, take a gamble with no risk, and be funny without being overfunny and to be liked in a reserved style—Freeze, Flight, or Frolic.

If this color is your lowest score then you might show these behaviors	If this is your highest score you might be	Early Warning Signal you sometimes come across as	Under Pressure you may even show the following behavior
Excitable	Even tempered	Easy going	Laid back
Gives in	Persistent	Incessant	Relentless
Intense	Easy going	Placid	Nonchalant
Solemn	Playful	Frisky	Mischievous
Outgoing	Dry	Deadpan	Sardonic
Orthodox	Unorthodox	Unusual	Eccentric
Similar	Different	Odd	Weird
Dull	Clever	Smart	Precocious
Unimaginative	Ingenious	Shrewd	Cunning
Makes mistakes	Accurate	Exacting	Precise

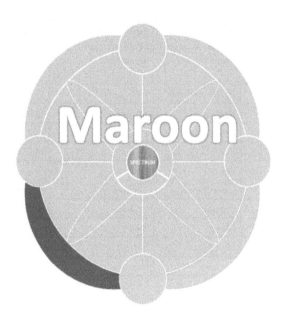

What if you have three scores that are equal. These are known as the Triple Blends and the first is equal scores of red, blue, and green (low yellow)—called Maroon.

You are likely to be more introvert than extrovert, and have everything in its place and a place for everything, but can lead and drive and confidently express yourself when you must in a calm and rational way, while striving to do things well and to a high standard.

Maroon is very hard and this is how you will be seen by others. You will have three counteracting values that will lead to some internal issues. Overall, you are seen by others as confident, competent, perfectionists, who are kind, firm, and state their views but can show emotions when they need to.

They can be task driven while delivering high-quality outputs and they can usually achieve more than most people would expect. They will do whatever anyone else cannot do to their standards and they will tell you to. They do not mean to hurt you but they will erupt when disappointed. Probably more extrovert than introvert, but when push comes to shove you might get some aggressive behavior—Fight, Freeze, and Flock.

If this color is your lowest score then you might show these behaviors	If this is your highest score you might be	Early Warning Signal you sometimes come across as	Under Pressure you may even show the following behavior
Divergent	Convergent	Narrow-minded	Singular
Task focused	Results driven	Quick to finish	Rushed
Messy and slack	Quality driven	Purist	Perfectionistic
Modest	Confident	Boasting	Bragging
Genial	Stern	Frowning	Severe
Half-hearted	Resolute	Driven	Unyielding
Irrational	Logical	Unemotional	Unfeeling
Inaccurate	Accurate	Clipped	Veracious
Unresponsive	Responsive	Speedy	Immediate
Impatient	Patient	Forgiving	Tolerant

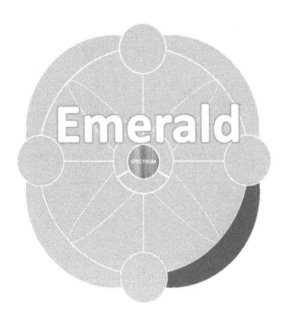

Next is Emerald, an equal mix of green, blue, and yellow (low or no red)—you are likely to be neither extrovert not introvert, but have the ability to work alone or in teams, striving for quality and methodically working your way through tasks, but able to use some humor in a dry way to express your opinion using an aside, sarcasm, or being rather sardonic.

You may bottle up your feelings and emotions until you explode in a torrent of anger, you will be a stickler for quality and detail but you could have the devil in your eye, your humor will save you on occasions, and you will enjoy having quality people and things around you. You are neat and tidy, but to a degree where you might be able to live with some mess. You will know where everything is, and you will like people and can equally be comfortable in large groups or with a small circle of intimate friends.

You will also be a team player and not necessarily leading it, probably more introvert than extrovert but you may also on occasions show some rare aggressive behaviors against your normal self—Freeze, Flight Frolic, or Flock.

If this color is your lowest score then you might show these behaviors	If this is your highest score you might be	Early Warning Signal you sometimes come across as	Under Pressure you may even show the following behavior
Telling	Asking	Requesting	Begging
Tough	Lenient	Soft	Malleable
Disloyal	Loyal	Serving	Slavish
Hard	Gentle	Humble	Benign
Careless	Careful	Economical	Thrifty
Uncontrolled	Controlled	Dominate	Master
Superficial	Thorough	Exhaustive	Assiduous
Repulsing	Charming	Smarmy	Obsequious
Unpopular	Popular	Sought after	Addictive
Rough	Polished	Slimy	Slippery

Another is magenta, an equal mix of blue, red, and yellow—you are likely to be more extrovert than introvert and have an ability to plan and use logic to solve problems in an innovative and decisive way. You might also have a good sense of humor and enjoy social events. Someone who enjoys planning and keeping things under control but with a wacky or wild side waiting to come out.

Unlike the flower, you will not be a shrinking violet. You will have all the attributes of controlling events, situations, and relationships; the humor, wit, and charm to pull this off; and need to complete tasks quickly combined with a subtle ability to plan and organize thoroughly and carefully with accuracy.

The detail is a means to an end; the charm is a way to get others to help and ultimately help you achieve your goals and ambitions. More extrovert than introvert, the main focus will be getting things done in a fun way and you may expect to get some playful and comedic behavior—Frolic, Fight, flight, or Freezing.

If this color is your lowest score then you might show these behaviors	If this is your highest score you might be	Early Warning Signal you sometimes come across as	Under Pressure you may even show the following behavior
Evasive	Direct	Straight to the point	Blunt
Unwilling	Eager	Fervent	Fanatical
Listless	Lively	Zappy	Exuberant
Boring	Entertaining	Silly	Daft
Rigid	Flexible	Pliable	Malleable
Moderate	Skillfully outrageous	Shocking	Scandalous
Chaotic	Methodical	Meticulous	Punctilious
Aimless	Medium-term planning	Prepared	Organized
Frivolous	Dry humor	Sarcastic	Wicked
Submissive	Forceful	Pushy	Bossy

Last of the three mixed colors is tan, an equal mix of red, yellow, and green (no or low blue)—you are likely to be more extrovert than introvert, outgoing and social, with a high level of confidence, and strive for high quality and excellence. Innovative, creative, and possibly with a hidden artistic nature, someone who likes people and being at the center of important things, also could have a naughty or mischievous side.

Tans come in all shapes and sizes and change color throughout the year and this is how folks are seen by the outside world. A driver, an entertainer, and someone who wants to do things well and be liked by everyone. They are more likely to be extrovert than introvert and probably team players and those who are happy to lead, steer, or at least air their views.

Winning or achieving is very important, so is having fun, but they are loyal too. Fun and lively with an impulsive nature, you like nice things but people might get bored easily and so you might expect some playful and humorous behavior—Fight, Flight, Frolic, or Flock.

If this color is your lowest score then you might show these behaviors	If this is your highest score you might be	Early Warning Signal you sometimes come across as	Under Pressure you may even show the following behavior
Calm	Excitable	Highly strung	Volatile
Safe	Risk taker	Gambler	Punter
Long-term planner	Short-term planner	Reactionary	Impulsive
Indirect	Direct to the point	Frank	Blunt
Intellectual	Physical	Playful	Frisky
Distant	Tactile	Touchy	Oversensitive
Tame	Wild	Outrageous	Shocking
Tactless	Tactful	Flatterer	Grovelling
Slow	Fast	Rapid	Blistering
Unfinished	Achieving things	Overfocused	Blinkered

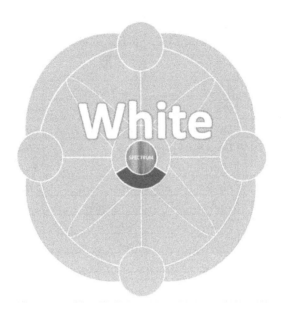

However, if your scores are all equal—what does that mean? This can only be determined by the online survey not the paper-based one, because this is how you score each question. Was it at the low end 0–1–2 or mid 3–4–5 or medium 6–7–8 or high 9 and 10? This then gives you a tonal color between white and gray, charcoal and spectrum (all).

The first is all low scores: White—you are likely to be introvert and very quiet, with a lack of confidence; you may even avoid social contact and will benefit from coaching and counseling.

White people would nearly be invisible and these profiles, where the scores are so low in all the colors, would be very rare indeed. I think these people would have very low self-esteem and not be very effective in many situations.

Quality things would not interest them and they would have little drive or determination, and no real ability to socialize or be humorous. They would have no plans and just live life day to day, hour to hour, and minute to minute, without any change, direction, or interests. They may appear to have suffered a lot and so you will often get a freeze and flight type of behavior, where they do nothing or run away and hide.

If this color is your lowest score then you might show these behaviors	If this is your highest score you might be	Early Warning Signal you sometimes come across as	Under Pressure you may even show the following behavior
Strong	Weak	Frail	Incapacitated
Stable	Unstable	Unsafe	Insecure
Emotional	Unemotional	Cold	Frigid
Active	Inactive	Idle	Lazy
Overstated	Understated	Underrate	Trivialize
Reacts	Never acts	Static	Unmoving
Confident	Lacks confidence	Distrusting	Skeptical
Exciting	Boring	Tedious	Colorless
Team player	A loner	Recluse	Antisocial
Eager	Apathetic	Indifferent	Languid

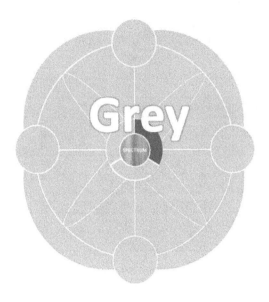

The second level or medium to low use of all behaviors is Gray—you are likely to be quite introvert and quiet and probably only speak when spoken to, perhaps a deep person who is difficult to read, and coaching or counselling will help you to achieve greater things.

Grey people would be just that, steady Eddie, WYSIWYG—what you see is what you get. Always dressed the same, even when they buy new things they just replace the old with the same. They won't like change, or modern technology, and although they have a desire to get on and have some quality around them, try to plan things, and make an impact, it would often be at the wrong time, in the wrong place, and with the wrong people.

They can be a bit insipid in a group—not standing out or been noticed much. So expect some mistakes at which behavior to use at the wrong time—Freeze and Flight and maybe Flock.

If this color is your lowest score then you might show these behaviors	If this is your highest score you might be	Early Warning Signal you sometimes come across as	Under Pressure you may even show the following behavior
Fast	Slow	Unhurried	Sedate
Variable	Steady	Static	Stubborn
Assertive	Passive	Docile	Subdued
Inspirational	Uninspiring	Dreary	Insipid
Obstinate	Submissive	Obedient	Yielding
Optimistic	Cynical	Skeptical	Pessimistic
Direct	Indirect	Deviating	Meandering
Harsh	Mild	Meek	Unassuming
Proud	Humble	Self-effacing	Apologetic
Decisive	Indecisive	Ambivalent	Dithering

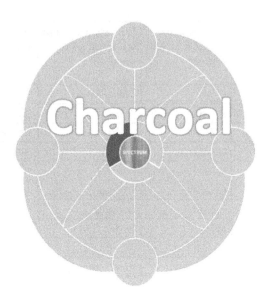

The next level or medium–high use of all four behaviors equally is Charcoal—You are likely to be neither introvert or extrovert and a deep thinker, who is difficult to read but often surprises others with unexpected actions or thoughts.

Charcoal is the fuel for barbecues and they are difficult to light but once they start burning they create an amazing amount of heat. While Charcoal scores are medium to high in all the colors and they might be difficult to motivate and get going on a project, but once enthused, they use these equal quantities of all the colors, they will be like a dog with a bone, and they will not let go until the job is done fast, well, and thoroughly. They usually make good managers or team leaders.

They can use the fight style if they must, they can flock when they need to, and they will freeze if it is appropriate. They are fairly good at using all the behaviors when they need to and at the right time.

If this color is your lowest score then you might show these behaviors	If this is your highest score you might be	Early Warning Signal you sometimes come across as	Under Pressure you may even show the following behavior
Insecure	Safe	Overprotected	Guarded
Closed	Open	Extensive	Exposed
Mean	Kind hearted	Overgenerous	Lavish
Avoiding	Answerable	Accountable	Liable
Biased	Neutral	Sits on the fence	Indecisive
Lenient	Strict	Harsh	Caged
Pessimistic	Optimistic	Hopeful	Dream land
Gives up	Tenacious	Immovable	Dogged
struggles	Manages	Copes	Survives
Fictitious	Factual	Word for word	Exacting
Unpredictable	Predictable	Expected	Unsurprising

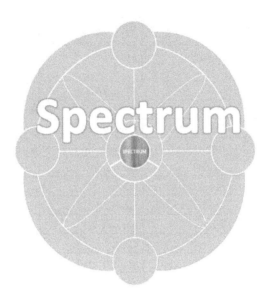

Finally, if your scores are all high and all 8–9–10 for every question and you were being honest about yourself, then you are Spectrum—a high user of all the colors equally—you are likely to be in great demand as an inspirational leader and someone with all-round talent for most things. If something interests you and you have a passion for it, you will achieve it. Using all the behaviors equally as the situation and role demand you are probably successful and if you are not—then you should be.

Spectrum is what everyone wants to be—this behavior is consistently using the right behavior, at the right time and in the right way, and these people are skilled in all areas of life. They do not need to get angry to get their way, they do not need to be stubborn to influence others. They use their wit and charm, all their behavior is under control, and everyone seems to like and trust them; they have it all.

They will be popular, in demand, and always asked for their opinions. Their score will be high across all four colors and they know where they are going, how to get there, who is coming with them, who they can trust, and are usually very successful in all areas of their lives. Their ability to use flock, fight, frolic, freeze, and flight at the exact right time is perfect. They rarely make mistakes. Everyone seems to like and admire them, and the sky is the limit as to where they can get to—please can I be one of these?

Please remember it must be found that a person who has the ideal spectrum profile needs to do a 360-degree report so that it is ensured that all others see this person in the same way—it is no good just thinking that you are brilliant at all behaviors if no one else does. You must be seen by all the others in your life—partner, family, social group, boss, staff, peers, clients, suppliers, and professional groups—as a wonderful user of behavior, inspirational leader, and one having that Wow Factor!

If this color is your lowest score then you might show these behaviors	If this is your highest score you might be	Early Warning Signal you sometimes come across as	Under Pressure you may even show the following behavior
Uninspiring	Inspirational leader	Goading	Inciting
Diffident	Confident and decisive	Cocky	Overbearing
Unaware	Conscious and aware	Oversensitive	Emotional
Hot headed	Cool and calm	Calculating	Cold and unemotional
Unknowing	Knowing	Cunning	Sly
Passive	Assertive	Forceful	Aggressive
Pessimistic	Optimistic	Buoyant	Bullish
Unforgiving	Forgiving	Merciful	Lenient
Inept	Gifted and talented	Consummate	Masterly
Disciple	Guru	Spiritual	Iconic
Makes mistakes	Quality driven	Flawless	Faultless
Rudderless	Motivational	Inducing	Forceful

Exercise—sit down and talk through your profile with someone who knows you and ask:

1. Am I like this?
2. Tell me when you have seen this?
3. Have you seen my stress colors and when did you last see it?

CHAPTER 9

Aim Behavior Consequences and Stress

In this chapter, we look at ABC, that is, your aims, your actual behavior used, and the consequences of using that behavior. We also look at the effect of stress on your colors. The analogy we use is twofold: one is an accelerator pedal and brake pedal on a car, to show how behavior either accelerates or slows down under stress, and the second is as if your behaviors were getting hotter or colder under pressure or stress.

So, behavior is nothing more than the words (content) that you use together with your facial mask, body language, voice, pitch, tone, and volume. Eighty percent of communication is nonverbal—If you do not believe me, turn the sound down on your telly and you still know what is going on in any film in any language. Remember a picture paints a thousand words.

Let me explore this just a little further. If you have the "appropriate" (what others expect of you in that situation and current role) facial expression, body language, and words, together with the right pitch, tone, and volume, people will say or think that it was "good behavior."

Get one of these wrong and people will think you are "too much" for the situation and you will appear, rude, gruff, arrogant, stubborn, sarcastic, sulky, silly, and so on. One classic example of this is sarcasm or dry wit. Everyone knows someone who is funny but keeps a dead pan face; the response from strangers is always, "Is he serious or joking?"

This is also known as the congruence; degree of match or similarity among aim, behavior, and consequence (ABC).

Aim—it is what you intend to achieve with your behavior: the preconscious moment before we use any behavior and created in milliseconds.

Behavior—how you behave and the degree of congruence you have with your use of facial expressions, voice pitch, tone and volume and content, together with the appropriate body language Used.

Consequence—it is how you think others receive and perceive your behaviors or the outcomes, the response you get from using this behavior, that is, laughter if you are telling a joke would be a success, and no laughter would be a failure.

If these are the same in most of the situations and roles that you play, then you will be a very effective communicator and get on well with other people and be seen as such by most people.

If, however, on occasions others are left confused as to what you mean and you feel frustrated at trying to get your message across, then it is likely that you have a difference between your aim—what you are trying to achieve, the behavior that you are trying to use to achieve that aim and consequence, and the result you actually get.

In simple terms, if you do not use the right behavior at the right time, with the right person, or people, then you will get the reaction you deserve.

As Aristotle said, "Anyone can become angry, that is easy. But to become angry with the right person, at the right time, in the right way and to achieve the right outcome, that is difficult."

The next level of understanding behavior is that you do have all the software at your disposal, every piece of behavior is available to you, free of charge, but through bad experiences, negative feedback, lack of praise or just failure, and lack of confidence to try, we have stopped using some of these behaviors or maybe never tried them in the first place. Again, humor is a good example of this; if we do something funny our reward is laughter, so we do more. If no one laughs and we feel that we have failed we may try a few more times but then give up and say, I cannot tell jokes or be funny so I do not even try.

So, by the time we are adults we have a preferred limited use of behaviors that work for us most of the time in most situations and relationships, but now again they don't work and we say, "Oops, I was too aggressive or too passive for that situation and I should have used a different approach."

When we feel under threat, in stress, or just uncomfortable with a situation, most of us keep using the same behaviors, only most of us use more of it. So for example a strong loud voice may head towards shouting if not understood. A bit like being abroad and trying to communicate with a German, a Frenchman, and a Spaniard, we can only speak English. We then slow down and get louder as if that will work! What we should really do is to pick up a phrase book and try speak in, German, French, and Spanish. To start with we are clumsy and make mistakes but with practice we can learn to speak any other language. Behavior is the same, we must try to use other unused, untried behaviors and, slowly, with practice become proficient at using other new behaviors. You can learn to use new, alternative, or different behaviors.

To show you the way in which most people continue to carry on using the same behaviors but excessively (more of the same) when an alternative is actually required, we use a thermometer as the analogy.

Our body is usually at 98.6°F, which is healthy. If your behavior is at body temperature then this means you are using good behaviors for the situation you are in. At 92° we are cold and dying and so are our behaviors if we use these inappropriate introvert approaches to certain situations. At 100° plus, we are ill, hot, and suffering a fever.

Imagine you are not in any stress, calm, and relaxed driving along a motorway and you are at the maximum speed, you will arrive at your destination at the correct time, and you would be using your normal or standard behaviors.

Now imagine that you suddenly hit a wall of traffic that causes you to be late, the stress levels rise, and you might, once the road clears, drive very fast, exceeding the speed limit, trying to catch up on time, risking your life and the lives of your passengers.

You might exit as soon as you can, find an alternative route, and get there safely but late.

You might cry, you might give up and go home, you might sulk, you might blame everyone else except yourself, or laugh it off with some humor.

Each of the colors tends to move under stress—stress for me is any change in the situation, role, or culture I am in or any changes to the behaviors of others, including their thoughts and feelings. This could be the trigger inside that suddenly causes changes in behavior for us or others. Now you must act—if you do not change, they probably will not or cannot and if you imagine that everything will be okay, or expect the better result without doing something, you are wrong. Act and act now.

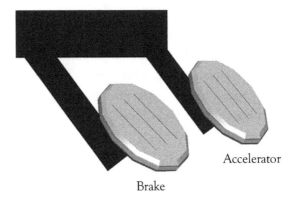

Accelerator

Brake

Roughly half the population press the accelerator pedal under stress and half press the brake pedal.

Reds and yellows tend to go faster under stress and blues and greens tend to go slower or press the brake.

Most people either use more of the same behavior (Accelerate) or less of the same behavior (Brake) under stress and pressure and what we are saying is why not try using a new or different behavior. The definition of madness is to keep doing the same things or behaving in the same way and expecting to get a different outcome or reaction from others—madness. Why not try an alternative way? Mirror, Signal, Maneuver is what we are taught when learning to drive so why not do the same with your behaviors – mirror the other persons volume, pitch, tone and content and body language and facial mask, and do it a little slower so it is obvious without patronizing or aping them.

Mirror the other person's style in what you deliver not mirror everything they say. So match what you do with what you think they want?

Signal—use different facial expressions and body language, pitch, tone, and volume to suit—signal to them that you are listening.

Maneuver—do what they want you to do as soon as possible. A few examples:

Reds—speed, action, and solutions quickly. Happy to be storming.

Blues—time to ponder, think, and come up with options at no/low pressure, would rather be in norming.

Greens—help and support, advice and assistance—like to perform to their best.

Yellows—a chance to shine and look good, to be at the center of everything—like forming new social groups.

The theory Forming/Storming/Norming/Performing comes from Bruce Tuckman (1965), who said that groups of people need to go through various stages of development in order to work as a team—when you put a group of people together as a new team, they will form into a natural team—seeking clarification and understanding of what is required of them. Then Storming takes place where arguments and infighting can ensue until a leader is found and people then know their place in the team. After a while the team will go into norming where everything is normal and we all do our tasks quietly and then as we get better at performing our tasks we can move into performing to the best of our abilities. Every time a team member leaves or someone new arrives, the team goes back into forming and storming for a short while and this explains why we love reality TV programs where the cast is constantly changed so that we see the storming every day and the stress is so high that we see excessive behaviors too—we love it.

Changing behavior is easy to say, and harder to do, but it works. Using the right behavior for the situation you are in and the role you are playing, to get the right outcome you wanted, is much harder!

A man flashes his lights in my rear-view mirror, as he wants to overtake but there is no room. So I could behave using a:

Red reaction—stick up two fingers, speed up, and let him try to catch me.

Blue reaction—slow down and stubbornly keep to the speed limit.

Green reaction—pull over and let him go by.

Yellow reaction—ignore him and hope he goes away.

So what did I do?

I did the red thing, but he caught me up as he had a sports car and after he had overtaken me, he pulled over blocking the road and got out of his car in a very aggressive and threatening way. I felt in danger. So what should I do next?

Red reaction—get out and have an argument that might lead to a fight.

Blue reaction—put car in reverse and try to exit the situation—run away.

Green reaction—apologize and keep saying sorry—three times sincerely with a genuine look on your face.

Yellow reaction—lock doors and do not make any eye contact, call the police, and hope he goes away eventually.

I did the green thing, and, guess what, after three times of saying sorry (even though he was at fault) he calmed down, lost all aggression, and was disarmed; he did not know what to do or say except, "OK well don't do it again." He got back into his car and drove off and not even very fast. Although some might argue I lost, I did not feel that I had, instead I felt empowered and in control and very good as I had controlled the situation and won by calming him down and not getting punched.

By the way I am not saying always back down. I have won using assertiveness too and the other approaches all work but in a different situation and at a different time you need to be able to move quickly from one color to another without compromising your beliefs or values.

However, beware of written behaviors—or text—as it has no pitch, tone, or volume and can be misread. Remember "I never said she stole my wallet" example earlier in the book.

Next, we need to look at stress and why we stay with one color in stress and use more of it instead of simply changing to another color. We need some levels of stress to be able to perform better and the first is Positive stress—when we get slightly better at everything, our senses are heightened and we become for a short period better at things—for example, playing sport, making a presentation for a sales pitch to a new client, or going on stage to play a part. Helping someone is stress or injury situation. Finding strength where we did not know we had it.

The next level is Negative stress—now we are under pressure and cannot seem to behave productively; use of our behaviors becomes too much and may move from confidence to cocky and onto arrogance, or from helpful to mothering to smothering, or from witty to silly to a clown, and maybe even from careful to thorough to nit-picking or unmoving.

There is also distress when a person cannot cope and needs emergency help. Be aware that if someone is using abnormal or atypical behaviors you should always refer them to a counselor, a general physician, or a psychiatrist. If someone is absent through stress remember that you would have seen the early warning signals in the days leading up to them being signed off work. Were they sighing at their desk, crying, losing their temper, shouting, clearing their desk, or exhibited some other unusual behavior? If they were, you should intervene; ask them if you can help? Or refer to their boss or human resources (HR). It is your duty.

So, stress is a trigger for our behaviors in most cases and it can arrive in the form of an unwanted change. Our reaction to change mostly is to either move up or down in our chosen behaviors; use less or more of the current ones being used—sometimes known as a temperature change: colder or hotter for the situation we find ourselves in.

Hotter—getting faster, louder, and noisier; closing the space between us and them; making stronger eye contact; becoming red faced; going toward the situation or person or event; and heading into rather than away from whatever is the cause, known as fight or frolic.

Colder—calmer, slower, more thoughtful, reflective, away from the situation or person or event, less eye contact or none, and becoming pale faced, maybe even running away or absent, known as flight or freeze.

Sometimes we just get warmer—getting everyone together sharing, all for one and one for all—known as flock which has a cosines to it and is a team player, inclusive and asking rather than telling.

Here are a few examples of how people tend to stick with same behaviors instead of changing or trying an alternative:

Base color	Positive use	Early warning to excess	Overuse/weakness
Red	Confidence	Cocky	Arrogant
Blue	Thorough	Analysis paralysis	Stubborn
Yellow	Witty	Silly	Clown Like
Green	Helpful	Motherly/fatherly	Interfering
Red	Competitive	Win at all costs	Cheats
Blue	Careful	Slow	Unmoving/pedantic
Yellow	Innovative	Constant changes	Latest state of incompletion
Green	Kind	Overgenerous	Goes without

In 1979 in the United Kingdom, we had high unemployment, the winter of discontent, and high inflation; a change, action, and a new leader were needed. The people of the United Kingdom voted for Margaret Thatcher who was by any analysis using red behaviors. Following her election to prime minister, started fixing things, challenging the unions and others and instead of thinking what color should she use to maintain these changes, keep everyone happy, and ask NOT tell others what to do (green behaviors), she used more of the same old red ones until we got an arrogant, aggressive style, which eventually got her sacked.

We are also like animals. We often do behave like a herd of animals, queueing or crowding, whether we live in villages, towns, and cities—congregating together. One animal we have more in common with than perhaps you first thought is the Zebra; zebra analogy comes from *Strategies of the Serengeti* by Stephen Berry 2006. It is a great book on the behavior of animals, how similar we are to animals on the Serengeti, and how organizations can mirror these behaviors. The herd animals are always moving to where it might rain tomorrow so that they have fresh drinking water. But under stress or pressure or threats of being attacked they tend to:

Flight—run away and hide

Fight—move toward in an aggressive manner (Margaret Thatcher's approach)

Frolic—mess about and play

Freeze—do nothing just freeze

Flock—move into the herd, back into the pack to be protected by the mass

We do the same; first consider children. Watch children in the classroom. A teacher tells little Billy off for not doing his homework in front of the whole class. Billy might run out of classroom crying and avoiding school or teacher, telling his parents he is ill the next day. This is Flight. Fight: have a go at the teacher—a growing response these days. Frolic: laugh and make a joke at the teacher's expense—humor or sarcastic. Freeze: say and does nothing just stares at the teacher until she or he stops or it subsides. Flock: the rest of the class come to Billy's aid by saying "it is not fair you always pick on Billy, leave him alone."

As we suffer pressure or stress at work we either get hotter and move toward a situation, relationship, or event that is stressing us out or we become colder and start moving away from the same situation, event, or relationship, or the third option is to freeze, to do nothing at all. So about 50 percent of the population get hotter under this stress, go faster, get angry, and/or even get violent when things are too hot to handle or the frustration we are feeling causes us to burst outward in a fit of rage and "throw our toys out of our prams" (clear the desk, shout at a colleague, or stomp out shouting and swearing).

The other 50 percent get colder and may run away—flight/freeze—and do nothing in the same situation, remaining stubborn, sulky, and uncommunicative—so while person A is screaming and shouting, person B might sit and stare at his or her laptop not moving or saying anything and even avoid eye contact. Others get up and leave, move away from conflict, and avoid the confrontation.

So, getting hotter means getting faster and more aggressive, and getting colder means getting slower and more passive. Fifty percent of the population usually go up the temperature scale when under threat, stress, pressure, or being unhappy, and these are usually the extroverts, and 50 percent usually go down the scale and these are usually the introverts.

There are of course early warning signals, clues that everyone gives out before this serious situation happens, but most of us are unaware of the these simple easy-to-see signs; we have learned to ignore these signs at our peril.

If you see or hear someone sigh—this could be or IS an early warning signal to internal frustration or a worry or a call for help. If a colleague slams the phone and mutters under his or her breath something they would not normally say—this is a sign. Illness and the "often" got a headache or just feels unwell is a sign too. Obviously, crying at work, having temper tantrums, being silent for long periods, being white faced or red faced, sweating, pacing, or being aggressive are just some of the behaviors no one should use; if these are used, they are asking for help and may not even know it themselves.

Early intervention here nearly always helps—"can I help you out?," "Are you ok?," "I can see you are not okay so what can I do to help?," may be enough to stop the progression to the next stage. There is some evidence in the United Kingdom that absence from work, and the absent-on-Mondays syndrome, can often be attributed to something that happened at work the previous week. An argument with a colleague, bullying, aggression, too much work, not coping, and so on. This could be enough to make someone wake up on a Monday and say I cannot go in today. How hard is it to go back to work once signed off with stress or depression? Some never return to that place of work but had someone (you) done something in its infancy it might have stopped it. You have the power to help others every day at work, even if that person is a boss and several pay grades above you. Being at the top in a business is a lonely place too and can be more stressful than that at all the other levels.

The next thing you need to know is that when we are under pressure, or in a stressful situation, or with someone who causes us to feel stressful, or there is a change to the situation we are in, or we are not getting what we want from a situation, initially we use our positive behaviors; at least at the start we do. We are trying to influence others to believe us, to listen, or for us to influence them in some way but if we fail for whatever reason we start to either increase or decrease the use of our main behavior or color. People with a red or yellow preference will accelerate or increase their behaviors and people with a preference for blue and green behaviors will slow down or brake (decelerate). Unfortunately, now others see our behavior as negative or excessive, too much for the situation we are in. Our aim may still be correct but our actual behaviors or the way we are seen by others is now considered excessive. If we keep using the same behaviors, then we must expect the same reaction.

We then do not get our way, or feel stressed, pressured, or threatened; so we use more of the same behavior forcing us up or down the scale, coming across to others as being awkward, annoying, angry, sarcastic, rude, nasty, defensive, or unhappy.

If we still do not get our way, we move up or down again and are now seen as completely aggressive or passive, and the only option left is to fight, freeze, flock, frolic, or flight.

But, in summary, we will, if push comes to shove, or the last straw breaks the camel's back, fight both verbally and physically, or freeze, and do nothing; flock with others and invite them to join their side with, "what do you think?," "You agree with me, don't you?"; or frolic, using behavior such as humor trying to reduce tension using wit, charm, friendship, and jokes. Finally, some run away "flight" trying to escape the issue, conflict, or problem.

Before we totally explode or implode at the very top or very bottom of the behavioral thermometer, we typically jump to other end of the scale and to the extreme and so very aggressive behavior; can suddenly become very passive, detached, stubborn, sulky, and uncommunicative displaying passive, inactive, silent, and conflict-avoiding behavior; or can suddenly become explosively aggressive. The final straw that breaks the camel's back is the last thing that anyone can tolerate and then they just explode.

So not only have you got the power to stop this through early intervention and helping someone as described earlier but the person himself or herself has a choice.

Do I continue to use more of this current behavior and go from assertive to cocky into arrogant, or from quiet and calm to stubborn and unmoving, or from funny to silly to daft or from helpful to mothering to smothering, or we can choose to use a different behavior at that moment—why continue using more of what is NOT working when I can use a new behavior that might just tip the balance in my favor.

I hope you get this—but if you still do not, this may help—imagine four people in the car, one of each of the four main primary colors or behaviors. Mr. Red is driving—well he would be or wouldn't he. Mr. Blue is the front-seat passenger and is the navigator using a map (yes I know everyone has Satellite navigation systems in cars. The two rear passengers are Mr. Green and Mr. Blue. Let us look at their motives and the behaviors they might be using to influence the others, all trying to achieve what they perceive is the right solution. The object is to drive 100 miles to attend a meeting with a client as a team and make a presentation worth millions to the company.

The journey takes two hours in average normal traffic and weather. Today it is raining and windy.

The boss of the team (Mr. Red) says, "Let's leave one hour and 50 minutes before the meeting starts, I will drive, I am in charge, I can drive a bit faster, cut a few corners, overtake a few cars, break the speed limit between speed cameras and even if we think we might arrive late, we can phone ahead and give them a reason."

Mr. Yellow says "Oh okay, whatever you say, I agree with, I will bring some music to listen to and I have done a quiz so we can have laugh on the way."

Mr. Blue says, "Are you sure that will be earlier enough, I wanted to get there one hour early and safely. What if there is traffic? I wanted to set up the room, have a practice and make sure all the technology works and take our time—I feel rushed and under rehearsed."

Mr. Yellow says, "Don't worry we will blag it."

Mr. Green, who has been sitting and listening to this, says, "I am worried about leaving it tight, I need to see the quality of the graphics on their screen before they do and ensure it looks and feels the same as it does in our office."

Mr. Red says, "Stop worrying, I had a quick look last night on my phone before I went to bed, it will be alright, I have been in this situation many times and so let me run with it, you guys chip in when you have to. Okay?"

And off they go, but they hit a wall of traffic as there has been an accident. Stress levels in the car rise.

Mr. Red, "Why didn't someone check the traffic before we left; now we are going to be late."

Mr. Blue, "I did tell you we should have left earlier and checked the route before we left."

Mr. Red, "Shut Up."

Mr. Yellow, "Oh well at least we will have more fun time together chatting won't we?"

Mr. Red, "Clear off and shut up."

Mr. Green, "It is all my fault, I should have said yesterday when I saw the weather forecast and could have spoken up at the rehearsal last week. I should have sent a copy ahead for them read in case we were late. Oh dear this is terrible."

Mr. Yellow, "What do we do now?"

Mr. Blue, "Let's phone ahead, tell them we are going to be late, take the next exit, find an alternative route and get their late, but safe."

Mr. Red, "I think we can drive up the hard shoulder, weave around a few cars, do a U turn over there, drive the wrong way up that road to the no entry sign, drive onto that grass verge and onto that side road and if I put my foot down we could still make it on time."

Mr. Green, "That's illegal, we might get arrested and into serious trouble."

Mr. Yellow, "Sounds like fun to me—let's vote on it."

Mr. Red is already driving the wrong way up a road … a flashing light and siren can be heard.

Mr. Blue and Mr. Green, "Oh dear"…

Alternatively, it could have gone like this:

Mr. Red, "I always go too fast and rush, Mr. Blue you are better at planning and Mr. Green is better at the quality on the slides. Mr. Yellow is the best presenter in the business. So, Mr. Green and Mr. Blue make sure the presentation is fine and check it in advance. Phone ahead and ask about the room and projector, and what kind of set up they have there. Mr. Yellow, once it is ready, you and I will have a practice run, with all of us giving feedback. Mr. Yellow you do the links and make it fun. Mr. Green and Mr. Blue do the detailed bits in the middle and I will do the start and ending okay? Ahead of that, Mr. Blue check out the journey times and the route and make sure you get me in the car in time—don't take no for an answer. Don't let me get side tracked, okay?"

He has changed his behaviors to suit the other three, but still kept control.

So, your personality reacts with a situation and creates an emotion/feeling based on the culture you are living in at that moment, and the role you are playing, and then decides whether to do the right or wrong thing, choose the good or bad option, and then exhibit that behavior through voice, pitch, tone, volume, eye contact, and body language, which others then judge us on. Our personality is the engine—then driving the personality are six basic emotions, which then drive our behaviors. Degrees of happiness, sadness, fear, anger, surprise, and disgust (Research by Glasgow University 2015) from these hundreds of secondary behaviors appear. We then add our colors to these basic emotions and this leads us on to "how we feel."

I believe that each emotion then drives a basic color or behavior so that others can see how we feel through our voices and faces and body language.

How to deal with a stressful situation, event, or relationship? Well there are only two ways: remove the issue or change your behaviors and theirs through friendly constructive feedback. And when unhappy with a situation that you are in and do not want to have a conflict use the escalation route, which is simply—(1) Ask naively, "Is that ok to …?" (2) "I am unhappy about … Please do something about it," and lastly (3) "If you do not … I will report that to …"

Positive basic emotion	RED	YELLOW	GREEN	BLUE
Happiness	Content to be getting on with things and winning, feeling that others are also achieving so I am happy.	Laughing, Joking and External-izing our joy, trying to infect others into how we feel—at the center of things.	Smiling and making good eye contact and in agreement with how things are going.	No threats or risks to my current situation and no changes around so I am content and feel that I am under no stress.
Fear	Assertive responses to fear, goes and confronts anything caus-ing fear and deals with it now! Counteracts fear with aggression.	Pretends not to be scared or in fear by making light of it and pushing others to the front to deal with it! Hides fear.	Shows fear in face openly, dis-cusses the fear with best friends and seeks advice and help from the closest allies.	Shows no fear, but instead goes into denial, and hides in doing things, like sending e-mails, buries head in work, and shows no fear
Disgust	Openly says what he/she thinks and says it to the person or people or team that have created the disgust—mainly rational—will over power others with volume!	Avoids conflict directly but instead uses sarcasm to say asides and sly comments and might beat around the bush—mainly emotional, Smiles out of context and incongruent with situation!	Always emotional, uses always and never statements, shows disgust with highly emotional statements, and shows these with strong values being pro-tected. Will Sigh!	Will write a stern letter or e-mail using pure logic, facts, and proof to show how disgusted they are with the situation and what needs to be done, uses back-door practices rather than face the person/people directly. Will Tut!
Sadness	Will go quiet—may not ever cry—keeps inside. This is a sign of weakness, so I will not let it out! Will say it is wrong, bad, and should not be allowed to happen. May show anger at injustices.	Will openly show emotion but may tend for the "happy" memories rather than the actual sadness. Will say let's try and remember when nit was better or when we were happy, cheer up!	Will show open emotion and cry in public to excess. Will use words like unfair, not fair, how is this justice for this to happen? This always happens to me and I could have done something to make it different if only I . . .!	Will hide emotion inside, all sadness is screwed down inside like a fizzy drink with the lid on it. Keep everything bottled up and is seen as quite hard and unfeeling, may say evidential things like, they smoked, drank, drove fast or had long-term illnesses and was likely to happen.

(*Continued*)

(Continued)

Anger	Aggressive, steps forwards, will not back down, increases posture, voice volume, and swearing maybe? Never admit defeat and will keep on going even if it is obvious that he or she has lost. Does not harbour grudges.	Sarcastic—conflict avoider, uses wit and charm to avoid fights but can be devious and clever at finding alternative ways to win with new methods and revenge. Remembers and seeks revenge.	Emotional, sulky, takes the blame, feels wounded, is responsible and accountable, and tries to be compassionate and fair—likes justice and truth. Gives in and feels guilty. Never forgets what the other party did and will bring it up—often!	Rational and firm and unemotional, uses evidence to prove it. Tenaciously keeps going until he or she stubbornly wins argument or changes situation. Unyielding—once finished it is finished. Never to be spoken about again.
Surprise	Animated and assertive, can attack—FIGHT	Animated, jumpy, shows surprise, and may move away/run away or make light of—FLIGHT/FROLIC	Will jump and show horror and be openly surprised and tell you how much you surprised them, will head towards others for protection—FLOCK	Will FREEZE and show less or no movement and then react later after cognitively assessing the situation. FREEZE.

CHAPTER 10

Changing Your Behaviors

It is nearly impossible to change your personality so why use personality tests at work? All they can do is tell about yourself and that is it. But you can change your behaviors easily and simply by thinking about it in advance, planning what you will do and how you will do it and then practice. Imagine you have an artist's pallet and on it is red, blue, green and yellow, white and black paint—did you know that from this pallet you can mix any color—any color at all. I believe that anyone can learn to use any behavior at all without compromising their beliefs or values. You can mix your voice, pitch, tone and volume, your eye contact and facial mask, and body language to use any behavior you want—it just takes practice. Try smiling now. You have just changed your behaviors. Try increasing your volume now, you have just increased your assertiveness and power. Remember you only do not have any power when you give it away or allow someone else to control you. Power comes from six key areas:

1. Physical Power—body language and your size (large people seem to have power even when they don't want it, and tall people are more likely to be employed than smaller people); so make yourself look bigger, stand up tall and puff your chest out, hold your head up, and make good eye contact. You can learn to increase this.

2. Personal Power—Natural gravitas is an ability to draw people toward you, to be liked and at the center of things. Watch those that you admire and that you think have this and copy them/mirror their style and behaviors. You can learn to copy those you respect and develop more power here too.

3. Professional Power—We admire judges, solicitors, doctors, and professionals, but try talking your job up. Every job is important and is required and is valued—so act like it. You can develop your professional power if you want to.

4. Positional Power—being a supervisor or a boss holds power, if my boss says jump, I say, how high. Be careful and respectful when you hold a position of power, do not wield it like an axe, but rather facilitate others keeping them on your side. You can try for promotion in most jobs.

5. Pounds—money—people with money have power; it is quite simple, and the more money they have the more influential and powerful they become—think Donald Trump. Most people can increase their financial situation.

6. Political Power—politicians have power and they seem to use it well. Some better than others. You can develop your small "p"—political power.

Tested and proved through social experiments in the 1950s and 1960s, psychologists like Skinner and Bandura, with "conditioning" you can train someone to react to anything, and the bobo doll, looking at whether fear is inbred or learned and whether aggression is transferred from adults to children. Children do not have fear when they are born; they learn it from their mothers or fathers, and aggression is also taught and copied—hence, show me the bully and I will show the bullied. Show me the father and I will show you the son.

Children are great, they have no fears, not scared to try things and do not know what is right and wrong and so they use gut feel or instinct— they are brilliant for the study of behavior, because they are learning from us and copying us, and they often get their behaviors wrong, they often use their behaviors excessively.

Then we tell them off saying things like stop behaving like that, don't do that, behave yourself or else, do that again and I will kill you. In fact, we are telling them off for copying us. Most children's behavior is copied from their role models, and guess who the number role model is? Yes, it is you. And when you get cross with your children, it is usually because they excessively use a piece of behavior which you have taught them or they have copied from you and it is now annoying you.

So, a piece of confidence that they copied from you or your partner is now being excessively used and is now seen by you as overconfident, cocky, or arrogant and so we tell them off. And worse than that we are giving them negative feedback and rarely praise. How often do you hear parents saying, "that was a lovely piece of behavior," or, "you behaved yourself today; well done."

We are taught as children, to treat others the way that we want to be treated, but this is wrong, we need to treat others the way they want to be treated.

How can we achieve this if we are not them?

And lastly you need to know, that to change anyone else's behavior you have to reward them or punish them, there is no other way.

So if a child; or adult, is exhibiting a piece of behavior that is blocking you in any way shape or form, the only way is to reward or punish it.

Let me test this with you and then you have a go.

What is reward? Well, praise, thanks, sweets, toys, love, affection, a cuddle, sex, a kiss, wages, a bonus, medals, certificates, merits, stars, promotion, employee of the month/year, a prize, and so on. Fifty percent of the population use their behaviors in a particular way to gain the above.

What is punishment or negative reward? Well that will be, smacking, shouting, telling off, taking toys and sweets away, isolation, prison, whipping, the death sentence, community service, the stocks, demotion, sacking, public humiliation, taking the micky, bullying, a threat, a danger, a risk, and so on. Once again 50 percent will deliberately use their behaviors to avoid these negative rewards or knowingly take risks with their behavior in the full knowledge that they could suffer the above.

So, the next time you see a parent rewarding a child for throwing their toys out of their pram and screaming and the parent gives them sweets to shut them up—you will see that they have positively rewarded a negative behavior and forever, that child believes that behaving like this will be rewarded. So, 20 years later in a team meeting, when the same person can't get their way, and they get cross, sulk, and throw their toys out of the pram, they are expecting to still get their way. When the manger rewards them with a "are you okay?" or a "Sorry" that is again rewarding bad behavior with a reward.

I also believe that nearly all human behavior is a deliberate attempt for a positive outcome for the person using it; in other words, all behavior at its very core is a selfish act to sub- or pre-consciously get what you want.

Again, please test this by throwing selfless acts at this notion. So even if you sacrifice yourself for someone else, it could be argued that you will receive praise and reward, a place in heaven; if you believe in God and so even this altruistic, apparent selfless act is done for self-gain, in a way. I cannot find a single act of behavior which does not have either a gain for doing it right for the "self" (me) or the removal of a threat or punishment.

I might go to church and give money to charity, I might do fund raising and I could be a governor at a school, all of these "acts" or behaviors are apparently good deeds so that others gain, but look deeper and you might find that by going to church I believe that god will find a place for me in the afterlife, I will get thanked for giving and collecting money for charities, I could even brag about it. That by being a governor I am making the school better for my children, having some control over their education and again I might get thanked or rewarded by the school, the community, or maybe like our chairman receive an MBE. By the way, not all the above applies to me personally, they are just examples. Less about altruism and more about you. When someone cries and says "I should have been there to help them." Who are they thinking about, the other person or themselves? Reward and Punishment. We all need both to be motivated and do anything including a change of behavior.

There was a very unethical experiment carried out in an American college in the 1970s, which today just could not happen, but it does demonstrate that you can influence another's behaviors by reward or punishment. They asked all the girls in a college, one at a time and without being able to talk to each other, and in a secret location, with just the bogus photographer present whether they would pose topless for a single snap with a Polaroid instant camera. It would never be seen by anyone else, nor would anyone else know that they had done it.

The opening gambit was thanks and praise and compliments about how pretty they were and what lovely bodies they had, 3 percent said yes on the strength of this positive reinforcement and his role in the university (power). Then the remaining 97 percent were offered cash on the table there and then, starting at $100 and another 12 percent agreed. The price was raised by a $100 at time until $1,000 was reached and at various stages many more agreed to pose. He even offered guaranteed passes in their exams if they did it. At this point I believe it was about

60 percent that had agreed and so the photographer then started to use negative rewards (threatened punishment) and threats and psychological punishments to entice them into the pose.

He said if you don't do it, I will tell your family that you did it anyway. Next he threatened to fail them in their exams.

Then to personally harm them or their families if they still refused. (How far can you go?) This was quite a nasty experiment and would not be allowed in today's society, but anyway by the end of the session—100 percent had agreed to pose. It was called by some as the "prostitution theory" (Lena Edlund, Columbia University) in that anyone will do anything if the price (reward) or punishment is enough. Threatened with death, most will do anything. Discuss this with others and see what reaction you get, ask them, "How much to pose naked?" or "steal something from a shop?" Don't tell them about this previous experiment or you will pre-programme their thoughts, instead just keep changing the reward and then punishment until they agree and they will.

By the way he never actually took any photos and the girls were told immediately afterward it was a set up and apologized to them.

The other thing with positive and negative rewards for behaviors is that parents, yes you. Parents get this wrong. To reinforce this here is one example of rewarding bad behavior that reinforces poor or unacceptable behavior into adult hood which you will all have seen and witnessed.

A 5-year-old child is screaming in a supermarket and behaving badly. It has literally thrown its "toys out of the pram/pushchair." Mum then tries to calm the child with kind words and cuddles but to no avail, so then gives the child some sweets to quieten them down and it works. Success? Or is it?

The child has now been rewarded for behaving badly, so the next time the child wants something it will repeat the behavior again hoping to get rewarded. Wind the clock forward 20 years and the same person is in a team meeting with you and some colleagues, and can't get his or her way. Metaphorically "throws toys out of the pram" and gets cross, raises their voice, and screams at another colleague. Colleague says "Sorry" the team goes quiet—no one punishes the behavior and in fact they have just reinforced it, as the person "GOT their Way" and they will repeat again next time—leaving us to all to deal with Mr. or Mrs. Angry (Red behaviors in excess) at work when under pressure or stress, a behavior learned in the supermarket 20 years before.

We know what behavior is; it is body language, your facial mask, eyes and voice pitch, tone, and volume, and where it comes from, we need a labeling device to describe simply and easily what the behaviors are, what they look like, and when they change. How and why do they change and then we need some help in improving our performance in using our behaviors more appropriately.

Personality	Situations	Role	Culture	Behaviors
- Who you are, what you believe your values spirit ethos.	- Where are you and what is happening around you- environmental factors.	- What is your role? what is their role?	- What is the national culture, local/reginal culture, what is the organizational culture, political, culture, family, street or sect?	- The words we use with apitch, tone and volume together with a facial mask, eye contact and expressions with body language, movement and animation
Who you are The deep beliefs Inherited What makes you tick	Ever Changing Phone Call E-Mail Comments	Job Role Family Role Social Role Friends Supplier Customer	Where you live Local rules Country Religion	Content Words Pitch, Tone, and Volume Facial Mask Body Language Eye Contact

CHAPTER 11

Style Recognition Exercises

In this chapter, we learn to look at others and really recognize and spot each and every color. With practice, getting your head up, eyes looking, ears listening, and retraining your sensing mechanism to feel others, you can become better at these and be more influential. For a successful relationship, role, or to handle any situation, you must treat others the way that they want to be treated and not the way you want to be treated; the only way to do this is for you to change and move toward their style a bit. They could also do the same and move toward your color.

So how do we change our behavior? There are only two or three ways to change any animal's behavior, and we are animals. Reward good behavior with praise, gifts, bonus, promotion, a raise, treats, thanks, and other rewards. Punish bad behavior with physical and/or mental punishment such as whipping, spanking, caning, hitting with the slipper, smacking, hitting, giving electric shocks, or torturing, all of which are now outlawed in our country. Negative rewards include demotion, putting someone on the naughty step, sending a child to his or her bed, being locked in a room, have toys taken away, sweets taken away, loss of earning or no bonus, telling them off, humiliation, shouting, rollicking, and so on. No matter how you wrap it up—unless we reward good behavior, and punish bad behavior—it does not change—it stays the same. And if you keep doing the same things, behaving in the same way as you always have—do not expect different results, do not be surprised when you get the same old behaviors thrown back at you. This is also the definition of madness—expecting the result to be different but by keeping on doing the same things. If you keep banging your head on the wall you will end up with a headache.

Our reaction to change is funny—when asked, most people say they want change until you impose it on them and then you get this predictable reaction to change based on their behavioral type. So, depending on your color you need to match their color to build rapport with them, match their values and beliefs, and then mirror their behaviors, and talk in their language. Here are some stories and case studies and some fun exercises designed to help you to:

How to:

- Recognize someone else's behaviors
- Identify what they need from you
- How to mirror and bridge toward their behaviors

Look at the words they are using—are they saying, "I, me, or we, or us"? Do they emphasize quality, speed, feel, and touch; do they say, "will" and is or "might" and "maybe"; and see if you can link these words to a color—initially try just four primaries and as you get more practice you will be able to use the secondary and tertiary colors or even the flat/level profiles. Keep it simple. Your first reaction to a color will be right.

Think of family members and profile them—if in doubt use the website. What color was your mother, father, brothers and sisters, and grandparents?

What about your friends, bosses over the years, members of your teams, your clients and customers, and even the colors of the company they work for? Easy?

Think of famous people. MPs, actors, sportsmen, and so on, and see if you can see their colors too. Look at others clothes, they usually wear their natural-choice colors unless it is a uniform or suit, but even then, they try to show their true colors in a watch, tie, socks, handbag, or something they drive, or use a gadget, or the way their diary is laid out or not. Look for the signs; they are there.

Here we have some fun stories that will help you to identify the color the person is using. See if you can see, hear, or identify the colors being used and change your behaviors to influence the people in these stories who are using excessive behaviors. Each one of these gives you the colors in a different way to show you that listening and looking as well seeing the numbers can lead you to a good assessment of another's behaviors and motives.

Case Study 1

Observation and Listening—OVER THE TOP! (try to read in the color and use the pitch tone and volume of each of the four main colors)

Scene

It is the July 1, 1916 and the first day of the Somme (One of the largest battles of the First World War, fought between July 1 and November 1, 1916 near the Somme River in France, it was also one of the bloodiest military battles in history.). It is 0600 hours. Gathered in a trench is the 1st battalion of the Dorset Light Infantry are waiting for the captain to blow his whistle to indicate all soldiers to attack and go, "over the top" (This is NOT a true story, it is for learning purposes only and is not meant to cause any offence to any soldiers who bravely lost their lives in the Great War 1914–18).

Each of the four regiments in four trenches has a Captain, Captain Green, Captain Red, Captain Blue, and Captain Yellow. Each one of the captains has less than five minutes to address his troops and get their morale and spirits up before going "over the top."

Captain Green (rather like Sergeant Wilson from Dads Army, John Coffey in the Green Mile, Leonard "Bones" McCoy or Nyota Uhura from Star Trek) who are predominantly Green, in voice pitch, tone, and volume, and are soft, gentle, and quiet people.

"Would you all mind awfully and gather round please? Thank you very much for coming. I hope you all had a jolly good night's sleep and that you had a lovely breakfast and are all comfortable now?

First of all can I say how lovely you all look; well turned out, smart and handsome and I am very proud of you all and it makes me feel quite emotional to see you all here now in front me. Now when the whistle goes, because it is very dangerous out and I don't want any of you get hurt, I will go first, whilst you all stay down in the trenches, whilst I check it out for you.

If it is very dangerous I will give-in and surrender and I will call you all forward to do the same, that way no one will get hurt. Now please do be careful on the barbed wire as it is very sharp and Watson snagged his trousers on it in rehearsals.

Good Luck, I will miss you all terribly."

Next Up is Captain Red (a cross between Margaret Thatcher, Donald Trump and Alan Sugar, Captain Kirk) Loud and arrogant.

"Now you lot get over here now. I am in charge and when I say run, you will run and you will fight and you will win, but it is not just about fighting or winning it is about being first, and so I am not waiting for the whistle, we will go now and use the act of surprise.

So, when I blow my whistle, charge okay? Right let's go and any namby-pambies will shot—by me—so get on with it, you useless tossers."

Next up is Captain Blue (aka the ex-health and safety officer with a voice a bit like John Major's, your science or maths teachers or Dr. Spok from Star Trek). Deadly serious, monotone, and boringly dull.

"Firstly, in precisely four minutes and 22 seconds, all 457 of us will hear a whistle and that whistle means, we have to go over the top of this trench and pursue the enemy by running at them at 4.8 miles per hour, on average, and firing approximately ten rounds per minute at the enemy. However, before any of this can take place I must check a few details."

"Secondly, before we go, I must insist that each one of you fills out in triplicate, form 11a, this stops you or your family from making any claim on me, should anything happen to you."

"Thirdly, you will all need to make a will, signed and witnessed by at least two others and handed to me before I can let you go."

"Fourthly, I must insist that everyone has a first aider with them at all times in case of injury. If we run short of first aiders, then I am afraid you cannot go."

"Fifthly, can you all take a high "vis" jacket so you can be seen, safety glasses so that no chards of glass, mud, or shrapnel can get into your eyes, gloves as the barbed wire is very sharp and toe-protectors to protect your feet."

"Sixthly, again before I can let anyone go, our Health and Safety officer, Reynolds, is going to plan and prepare for a pre-over-the-top visit, to ensure that all the trenches are safe, to check for and report on any hazards and he will make his presentation in writing and on Power-Point at 1800 hours and after that all necessary changes to the plan will discussed tomorrow."

"What did you say Smithers? Whistle, what whistle? That whistle sounds to me as if it is above the regulation 8 decibels, Reynolds get that whistle measured."

"Seventhly, … where is everyone …?"

Last to go is Captain Yellow; think Tony Blair, Chris Evans, Jack Black, Jim Carey, Jean Wilder, and all mixed together, laughing and smiling throughout wanting to entertain everyone with their wit and charm.

"Hi, chaps and chapesses, after all we are all friends, aren't we? When the buzzer goes, I want us to huddle around for a group hug and wish each other luck and just remember I will be right behind you."

"I want everyone to be happy with the plan and input into it, and so for the next few mins can we all split into focus groups, each with a nominated facilitator to discuss the strengths and weaknesses of this 'over the top' plan. We will then get each group to present their ideas and then vote on the best."

"I have some pre-over the top awards to hand out, and some chocolates for cook and lastly last one in the Germans trench is a sissy."

Case Study 2—Reading between the Lines

Looking at the content, words, and then reading between the lines, see if you can spot the colors emerge—this is a true story. If you were there what could you do to influence everyone else in the room?

$100M (£50M)—52-week internal refurbishment of a 12-story 1970s style office building with apartments on top floors and retail at the bottom and is modernized from rented flats to luxury apartments, niche shops, and offices with car parking underneath.

The project involves the removal of all existing fixtures, fittings, services, and so on; and installation of new partitioning, raised floors, suspended ceilings, air conditioning, public health services, lighting/power and finishing's, and so on, to create a modern office environment. It has luxury apartments on top and a posh retail outlet at ground level (Bose, Barbour, Brassier Blanc, and so on). Substantial structural strengthening is required to accommodate increased floor loadings and a basement car park.

Twelve weeks into the program, the project is already three weeks behind schedule and progressively getting worse.

Everyone is blaming everyone else for the slowness of this project.

At a recent site meeting, sitting around the table were: the Client, Architect, Services Consultant (M/E/PH), Structural Engineer, Q.S., and Contractor.

The Architect opens the meeting (smiling and jokingly)

"Well how is everyone? Good to see you all again. There are a few things we need to discuss concerning the programme. I would like to start by saying that despite some of the problems, which I am sure we can sort out, everyone is working well together."

Client ... Stern but quite quiet to start with.

"Well actually I am not very happy. In fact, I am very disappointed. The project is already behind programme and not only was I hoping for a very high quality building but expecting it to be finished on time. On top of all this I thought I was going to be consulted when problems arose and involved with this team in helping to solve the problems. Actually, I feel that I have been excluded so far."

Contractor ... Angrily

"I hope you're not blaming me. I am not going into any detail but you keep making changes and adding extras and information is frequently late. How am I supposed to keep to the original programme? Not only are we going to be late but all the changes you have made and all these delays will bring additional costs."

Client ... Emotional

"There is no more money and it is not fair to expect me to come up with more, a price is a price."

Quantity Surveyor ... Monotone and quite slow

"I have listened to the arguments and have been weighing up the options over the last few days and have come up with three alternatives. I have prepared a report and have included some figures which I believe to be accurate."

"One is to go back to the original design and program, thus excluding any extra work but still incurring the present time deficit and some additional costs which I have calculated and have a copy for each of you here."

"Secondly, we could stick with the new design and program and accept the extra costs, which you will see are included in the second paragraph of my report."

"Lastly, to go away and analyze the new design and program, make some adjustments to timings and specifications which I believe will incur some additional costs and take a bit more time, but not as much as the current schedule will. I have been unable to include accurate costings of this third alternative in my report as I do not have enough information on which to do the calculations, however, if you could let me have a few days I could come up with a true figure."

Services Consultant ... very angrily

"There is no point in you doing any more work as no changes are acceptable to my plans. My company is not prepared to compromise on the detail. I took a long time coming up with the right way to do this job and I am not going to change it and then run the risk of the building not meeting the occupier's specific requirements."

Contractor ... matching the anger

"I have been in this situation many times. I think you should let me run with it on my own. I can't make any promises, but if I push the subcontractors and everyone else to the limit and really put my foot down, I think I can save some time, hopefully reduce the extra costs and get the project back on line again. The main problem here is that we spend too much time in meetings discussing the problems, instead of getting out there, rolling up our sleeves and getting on with it."

Architect ... trying to laugh it off and waving his arms in the air in surrender motions

"Listen I know how you all feel, but isn't it always better to work as a team, collectively agreeing the best plan of attack at each stage."

"Do you think it would be a good idea if for the next ten days or so we meet every morning at say nine o'clock for a quick cup of tea and a bacon sandwich to discuss the previous day's work and go over what we expect to achieve on the current day?"

"Hey, we could even get a lap top computer to record the information, so that we can all have access to it at any stage and if we all swap mobile phone numbers as well, we can keep in contact all the time. I know this is a difficult project but if we all try to get on and stop bickering, I am sure we can all work this out to everyone's satisfaction."

Services Consultant ... gets up as if to leave

"I haven't any time for more meetings, besides we agreed the procedures at the start of this job and we should stick to them. I am short of people and the budget won't allow me to increase my input into this project. I am already losing money on this piece of work."

Client ... very stern now

"This is an important project for my company and it is our money. We are the customer and you are the supplier. If you can't do the job, just say so and we will either run it ourselves or find others we can trust to do things the way we want them done."

Structural Engineer ... sulkily and quiet

Who has been listening intently to the discussion and making copious notes finally states his position:

"The structural work here is critical and must follow a set sequence. I took great pains to produce very detailed drawings and now we have to check everything meticulously stage by stage during the construction."

"We set extremely high standards and expect everyone else to do the same. If we have made changes then it has been unavoidable and was to maintain these standards. I have previously been critical of some of the compromises on quality others seem to be prepared to accept. I must make it clear that I cannot make any further concessions."

Objectives:

1. Can you identify the preferred colors most used. Do not overanalyze and you only have content to look at 3 percent, you do not have pitch, tone, and volume, or body language so be careful not to read as aggressive if it is not being aggressive—watch out (not all) being used by each of the representatives?
2. What color change will you use to build rapport, calm down each party, and create the best win–win situation for all parties?
3. Write and be prepared to read out your next statement based on the aforementioned. Also be ready to explain the rationale behind your approach.

Case Study 3

What about using it for recruitment? Rather than employ someone who is like you, and we have evidence that we tend to choose to recruit people who are like us behaviorally rather than having the skills for the job, fit behaviorally, or bring behaviors we do not yet have. So, assume you had not met any of these people and were given their SPECTRUM scores, what could you deduce from their numbers?

A global electrical well-known brand was trying to launch a new innovative consumer product. The leadership team comprised of six people and all good at what they did. The sixth member and leader of the team had recently been head hunted by a rival company to make this company fail in hitting their deadline of launching at Christmas and against a similar product. The company knew that it would take three months to find an alternative Boss and so they decided to recruit from within the team. This they felt would cause minimum disruption. All the team members had been through SPECTRUM recently and the scores are printed in the table that follows. Remember that the individual will move into his or her unfamiliar profile for the first three months. Here is a summary of the situation with the SPECTRUM scores and some questions that need to be answered. The Organization must appoint a Brand Manager for a new Brand. There are five internal candidates. The successful candidate must manage the unsuccessful candidates. Each of them is regarded as being highly competent. You will be asked to prepare a report on all the candidates based on their SPECTRUM profiles only in percentages, which are detailed as follows:

In your report, you should include:

1. The current roles, which are finance, personnel (HR), sales, and marketing, then logistics (operations to retail outlets) and production line (getting it ready and in the right place—warehouse). Can you tell who does what job?
2. Who would you appoint based on these scores?
3. What will be the reaction of the others?
4. The difficulties that they might experience in the role.
5. The colors they should adopt to successfully deal with each of the other Managers and the entire group and remember this time you only have the data, you DO NOT have body language, face eyes, nor pitch, tone, and volume, or the content of what anyone might say!
6. Coaching and training needs for the individuals and the team.

	Green	Red	Blue	Yellow
BILL	36	14	30	20
HELEN	12	40	38	10
ANNA	36	18	08	38
FREDA	23	28	26	23
PETER	10	35	45	10

Answers—did you get them right based on the above color profiles?

Peter was Finance Manager—highest blue, and this is required for this role with a backup of red so that he can make decisions and oversee his team. Bill was HR (personnel)—high Green is essential for HR and high Blue for compliance to rules and regulations. Helen was Logistics Manager (Operations)—High red—she hits deadlines and delivers on time and to budget and is task focused. Anna was Sales and Marketing Manager—High yellow and Green—she was people focused. Freda was Production Manager—fairly flat profile—task focused and people focused and flexible to change. They appointed Freda as the brand manager for two reasons—one—she had the widest view of the end-to-end operations and interacted with all the other team members more than anyone else. And two—behavioral flexibility—the easiest ability to use all behaviors without huge changes or time. It was successful (an electrical product that had to launch before Christmas and beat a rival; to be first to hit the high streets). Peter quit because he thought he should have the job but went to a rival and is still head of finance on one brand.

CHAPTER 12

How to be More Effective

In this chapter I look at core competencies of an employee and these are usually summarized by the ability to lead, manage, present, work in teams, influence, reduce pressure and increase motivation, and sell; there are many others but I think these are the key ones that affect performance.

Leadership

To be an effective leader you need to be able to inspire people, drive actions, make decisions, solve problems, and delegate, as well as give and receive feedback from all staff at all levels and communicate well. But can this only be done with red? No, anyone can lead; they just need to use a different approach or style and does that make them less effective? Again, no. Any one of the colors can lead; it is not just about telling people what to do, it could be to ask, or facilitate, coach, mentor, and even lead by example. Is every successful leader Red? Name the top ten leaders in the world or the ones you admire the most and try to color profile them. Is Richard Branson Red?

In the Fortune Top 50 they said that these are some of the top leaders up to 2014.

- Pope Francis—has green and red in his profile. "Pope Francis has electrified the church and attracted legions of non-Catholic admirers by energetically setting a new direction. He has refused to occupy the palatial papal apartments, has washed the feet of a female Muslim prisoner, is driven around Rome in a Ford Focus, and famously asked 'Who am I to judge?'"

- Angela Merkel—blue, red, and green. Merkel may be the most successful national leader in the world today. She is, practically speaking, the leader of the European Union (EU), which is the world's largest economy, and Merkel has held that position for almost nine years. She played the lead role in managing Europe's debt crisis, keeping the EU intact while setting even Greece on the road to recovery.
- Alan Mulally, chief executive officer (CEO) of Ford—yellow, red, and green too. Miracle worker who saved the company without resorting to bankruptcy or bailouts by doing what previous leaders had tried and failed to do: change Ford's risk-averse, reality-denying, Cover your arse (CYA)-based culture. After earning $7.2 billion of profit last year—far more than General Motors—the company paid its 47,000 Union of Allied Workers (UAW) workers a record $8,800 each in profit sharing.
- Warren Buffett—CEO, Berkshire Hathaway—green and yellow. While lauded as an investor, Buffett also leads 300,000 employees with a values-based, hands-off style that gives managers wide leeway and incentives like owners. The result is America's fifth-most-valuable company. His influence extends much further than that, though: The world looks to the "Oracle of Omaha" for guidance on investing, the economy, taxes, management, philanthropy, and more.
- Aung San Suu Kyi—Age: 68 years—Chair, National League for Democracy—green and blue. The Nobel Peace Prize winner gave up freedom and a life with her family in Britain to protest military rule in Burma (now Myanmar). But nearly two decades of house arrest could not quash the opposition leader's determination. Since Suu Kyi's 2010 release, her political party has clinched dozens of seats in Parliament. Current law bars a presidential run in 2015; even that may change before long.

- Gen. Joe Dunford—Age: 58 years—Commander, U.S. Forces, Afghanistan—red, blue, and green. The Marine four-star general and leader of North Atlantic Treaty Organization's (NATO) coalition in Afghanistan "is probably the most complete warrior-statesman wearing a uniform today," says a former marine commandant. Dunford tells *Fortune* that his first battalion commander told him the three rules to success. The first? Surround yourself with good people. "Over the years," says Dunford, "I've forgotten the other two."

- Dalai Lama—Age: 78 years—Spiritual leader of the Tibetan people—green. For over 50 years he has campaigned tirelessly for peace, nonviolence, democracy, and reconciliation, especially among world religions; he has met countless times with popes, rabbis, imams, and others to find common ground. Winner of the 1989 Nobel Peace Prize, Dalai Lama radiates charisma. As for his influence, just ask those who look for his guidance on Twitter. All 8.6 million of them.

- Derek Jeter—Age: 39 years—Shortstop and captain, New York Yankees—green, blue, and red. As he began his 20th and final season in pinstripes, Jeter remains the type of role-model player that even a red Sox fan must grudgingly respect. It is not the five World Series rings he has won or his team record for career hits. In a steroid-tainted, reality-TV era, Jeter, the son of two Army veterans, continues to stand out because of his old-school approach: Never offer excuses or give less than maximum effort.

Spectrum leadership styles

Leadership functions	Green	Red	Blue	Yellow
Instilling a mission or purpose for the people	Share values and beliefs—we are together as one	Tell everyone what we need to achieve	Explain the importance of shared goals and visions, mission, and purpose in detailed documents	Get everyone to join in, have fun, build consensus, a collective responsibility for what the people want
Driving performance	Inspire people to head toward it and follow me!	Express urgency, turnover and profit, continuous performance improvement expectations of everyone	Uses detailed plans and documents and charts for performance using data and historical performance	Show people what it might look like when we get there, visionary presentations and pictures
Decision making	Collaboration and best way forwards but refers upwards if stuck—nothing is better than getting it wrong.	Tell everyone what to do—and doing something is better than nothing	Review all options and carefully pick the right one—doing nothing is better than something	Announce constant changes and short-term plans and revise it—doing everything and anything is better than nothing
Problem solving	Creative group participation	My way or the highway	Analysis data evaluation and options, moving forwards one step at a time, and reviewing where we have been	Experiment and play innovation and fun

Delegation	Trusting you shows patience and helping/coaching style—does it with you	Assume you can do it, with no/low supervision—leave alone but if wrong rebuke!	Give lots of details and the manual "how to" guide step by step instructions to teach	Invite others to join in, expect you to take on new tasks without being asked, show your initiative, and very informal, anything achieved will be added to your normal list of duties!
Giving and receiving feedback	Kind, helpful, considerate, constructive	Rewards success points out failures and can be destructive	Focus on negatives and uses data to prove points, objective, and are unemotional.	Positive and funny, use informal sarcastic chat to let you know when not good enough or below standard–cutting remarks!
Communication and information	Shares everything he/she can with everyone equally	Tell people the headlines now and again	Provides written information at regular intervals	Keeps in touch informally, networks with many

How to Make an Effective Presentation Using Spectrum?

When you stand up in front of a dozen or in some cases hundreds of people, your mouth goes dry, you shake, you feel physically sick, nerves kick in, and what happens next will define your success—can you overcome these or succumb to them?

I believe that if you prepare properly (blue), practice enough times in front of a video camera (yellow), get feedback from colleagues beforehand (green), and then use red behaviors to grasp the situation and "go for it," you will overcome the nerves and here is how.

Structure your presentation using and considering all the colors as mentioned previously.

Effective Presentations – mixing structure with style		SPECTRUM
INTRO	Start with a bang	RED YELLOW
SIGNPOSTS	Where is this going? What are you going to say?	BLUE
MAINS	Remeber the power of 3s	RED BLUE
SUMMARY	Linked to signposts and picking out the hardest hitting facts	RED BLUE
CONCLUSION	Linked to the beginning. Thing about questions and what you want to happen next	BLUE GREEN

Then—think about your audience—who are they? Is there a color preference in the room? What do they need and want from you? What should I put in it to turn them on and how should I deliver it? What style or color would be best?

What can I do to change? Mirror and Bridge toward my audience? Presentations are about creating an opening "bang," then creating interesting content, engaging the audience, and making it memorable. But it is more important to focus on the audience than yourself, and to talk to them in their language not yours. So, mirror it in your presentations, match their values with your content, and sell it to them in their language.

My Spectrum – GREEN

Productive Use	Excessive Use
Wants to present the participants with a "High quality" event	Reluctant to apply pressure
Wants to benefit the participants	Can become too involved
Takes participants at face value	Can be manipulated and become disillusioned
Makes allowance for participants	Feels sorry for participants
Makes participants feel important	Says YES rather than let anyone down

My Spectrum – RED

Productive Use	Excessive Use
Likes to be in total control	May dominate and TELL
Quick to act and urgent	May opt for action over thought and create pressure
Enjoys the challenge of a difficult situation	Can be too assertive and pushy
Quick to move in and seize and opportunity	Ties to force participants into action
Probes and presses	Makes participants feel uncomfortable

My Spectrum – BLUE

Productive Use	Excessive Use
Uses and manages data, fact and logic	Too much detail
Details the trade offs and options	Too slow
Highlights benefits Methodical	Monotone
Stable and consistent – no surprises	No flexibility on timings
	Not engaging with audience

What type of Voice—use their words and use their pitch, tone, and volume, but beware of shouting back or using too much volume.

My Spectrum — YELLOW

Productive Use	Excessive Use
Charming, smiley and engaging	Too much "show"
Sensitive to audience expectations	Not enough information
Flexible and experimental	May sound insincere
Likes new ideas — multiformat	May oversell or over emphasize

Body Language—mirror or copy it as far as you can but not mimicking it.

What about Selling?

What does Mr. Red want?—a quick fast service now; no fuss, no bother, and let us just haggle over the price I am going to pay. Does it go the fastest?

What about Mr. Green?—High-quality, well-made, great customer service and aftercare, and easy-to-use helpline/desk; project inclusion and regular updates. Is it the best?

Mr. Blue—options, costs, detail, the handbook, time to consider his decision, no pressure. Is it the cheapest? What if I want to return it?

Mr. Yellow—wants a relationship, needs to feel that he looks good? Will he get all the credit later? Can he be flexible about how he pays? Will it make him look good?

What about profiling your customers and your products or services? Matching your products to the buyer will increase your sales. For most the expensive and best products, aim at Greens. For latest innovative gadgets, aim at yellows. For safest, tried and tested products at sensible prices, aim at Blues. For something that has status attached to it, the fastest, biggest and most powerful, aim at Reds.

We can us the colors to identify how teams or departments in organizations or whole organizations operate too. This is very simple to do and can be very effective at understanding your culture.

Is your organization internally focused on its product systems and how it does things, procedures, and so on, or externally focused on its client's customers and the service it provides?

Externally focused

Internally focused

Next is the organization mainly focused on the achievement and mea-
surement of tasks (centralized) or on how people get on in their teams and
people it employs (decentralized).

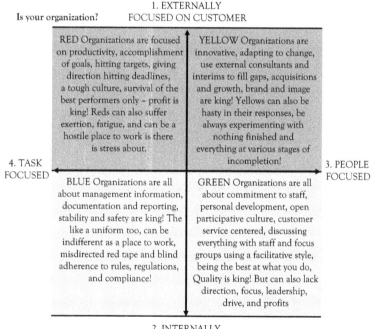

1. EXTERNALLY
Is your organization?   FOCUSED ON CUSTOMER

RED Organizations are focused on productivity, accomplishment of goals, hitting targets, giving direction hitting deadlines, a tough culture, survival of the best performers only – profit is king! Reds can also suffer exertion, fatigue, and can be a hostile place to work is there is stress about.

YELLOW Organizations are innovative, adapting to change, use external consultants and interims to fill gaps, acquisitions and growth, brand and image are king! Yellows can also be hasty in their responses, be always experimenting with nothing finished and everything at various stages of incompletion!

4. TASK FOCUSED

3. PEOPLE FOCUSED

BLUE Organizations are all about management information, documentation and reporting, stability and safety are king! The like a uniform too, can be indifferent as a place to work, misdirected red tape and blind adherence to rules, regulations, and compliance!

GREEN Organizations are all about commitment to staff, personal development, open participative culture, customer service centered, discussing everything with staff and focus groups using a facilitative style, being the best at what you do, Quality is king! But can also lack direction, focus, leadership, drive, and profits

2. INTERNALLY
FOCUSED ON PRODUCT, SERVICE, OR PROCESS

Red Teams and departments or organizations maximize production,
direct the action, are competitive, are in control, and are usually toward
centralization and short time frames. For example, logistics, Courier
services, investment banking, and production lines could have this too.

Yellow Teams or departments and organizations adapt and experiment involving others, have new ideas and creativity, introduce new products challenging the status quo, and are usually decentralized but with short time frames, for example, information technology (IT) and tablets, Apps, gaming software, marketing and advertising, and holiday companies.

Greens invest in training and people, develop behaviors and service to customers, valuing their ideals and ideas, are internally focused on how to make the quality of what we do better all the time, and are decentralized with longer time frames. Colleges, Universities, Hospitals, human resources, and service sectors.

Blue organizations, teams, and departments are centralized on measuring everything we do by the book, rules, policies, procedures, research, measurements, time tables, safety, and with very long time lines where planning is paramount and so is reporting. Railways, Metro and Underground, Bus and coach companies, Research and testing labs, construction industry, and so on.

There are Organizational Colors by Sector and within each organization by departments too and so here are a few:

- Finanace and Banking—Blue in banks but red in Investments!
- IT—Blue and Green
- Oil and Gas—Blue (engineering and pumping, health and safety, and yellow/Blue for exploration).
- Government—a mix, but local government is blue/green—following rules and regulations and making our lives better, ecology and recycling. Central government—red and yellow—get one's message across, new ideas, inspiring confidence.
- Health care—must be green and blue—kind, considerate, helpful, caring, needs the detail and analysis, diagnostics, and treatment.
- Manufacturing—blue and green—making stuff, maintaining quality, attention to detail, error free, but red and yellow for marketing and sales.

- Wholesale and retail—blue, red, and green, and some yellow in customer-facing roles.
- Transport and logistics—mainly blue and green—uniforms, compliance, highway code, time tables but also comfort of passengers and safety.
- Construction Industry—Blue and Green—health and safety building to specification and rules, measurements, and accuracy.
- Education—Green and Blue—needs quality, detail, facts and figures, proof, an ability to remember and recall, research statistics, methods, science, math, languages, geography, & history. Great tutors also use some yellow to make learning fun and red to create impact.

Then within each sector you have departments that also have a preference of using a color or a mix of colors.

- Marketing—yellow—innovative and creative, eye catching, and impactful.
- Sales—red and yellow—targets driven, pressure to succeed, all about turnover and income.
- Finance—blue—accuracy, detail, spreadsheets, error-free reporting.
- HR—wages and welfare, pensions, and so on—blue—accuracy; Business partners (BPs)—red—timely interventions; HR advisers—green—help and support and advice; Trainers—yellow—entertaining, witty, and funny, lively too. Employee realtions (ER)—blue—to the rules, by the book to the employment act and laws. Engagement, Communication, Rewards, and Recognition—green and yellow—it is all about people.
- IT department —blue—all must work all the time.
- Operations—red—hitting deadlines.
- Aftercare and customer service—green and red—quick fix, understanding empathy, and listening followed by action.
- Admin—green and blue—detail, error free, accurate, helpful, and supportive.

So, simply hand your work in the style of the next internal customer and the transition between teams will improve.

Marketing to Sales—what do they want to know and when, fast paced, high energy, and minimum detail. No fluff and waffle. When we say quick we mean now. Project cycles: 12 months.

Sales to Operations—enough detail with no mistakes, clear and concise instructions/order easy to follow and understand. Price, date, deadline, and quality needed. No detailed reports please—headlines only. What is it we are doing, when does the customer want, to where do they want it, and lastly how much are we charging? When we say quick we mean today. Project cycles—one week.

Sales to Finance—all the details on costs and to an agreed date and time with no errors in a format that we want, for example, Excel spreadsheet of our design with all boxes completed and not in crayon on back of piece of paper or by phone or verbally in the kitchen. Place on top of in-tray and leave me alone to process it. Allow us time to do it right. When we say quick we mean within one to four weeks. Project cycle: one year.

HR to all teams—ask, don't tell, what can we do to help? No/Low pressure is possible. Allow us Time to get it perfect. When we say quick we mean when it suits you. Project cycle: three months.

IT—by e-mail to inbox, then allow seven days as we are behind on our work loads, no sudden change please, and as much advanced warning of help you may need. When we say quick response, we mean a day to a week. Project cycle: minimum one year and always three months late.

Aftercare and Customer Service—to external customer—as fast as possible project cycle now. Or within one day—seven days max. By phone/e-mail, and so on.

What About Profiling Whole Organizations?

We can profile your team or whole organization using Spectrum—and create group, team, or organizational reports; this is very powerful for many reasons but mainly because a lot of organizations employ people like themselves—I like me so I will like someone who uses similar behaviors but when faced with change the "one style" approach leaves the team short of the behaviors required to get them through change.

This is the profile of an organization in 2013. After they had been trained in SPECTRUM they recognized that in stress everyone hid. It shifted slightly from an AQUA style in normal situations to Blue in stress. So, everyone went quiet in stress, with silence, head down, and e-mailed each other—even if sitting next to the person you wanted to communicate with—by the way I think excessive e-mails in an organization usually shows a sign of arse covering or finger pointing going on.

The leadership team then trained people to use more and wider behaviors; they even started employing people not like the ones they already had, and who were different under stress so that they could reduce the amount of blue in stress they showed when under pressure, which was there most of the time. They achieved this and people became more challenging and more outspoken, able to cope with change.

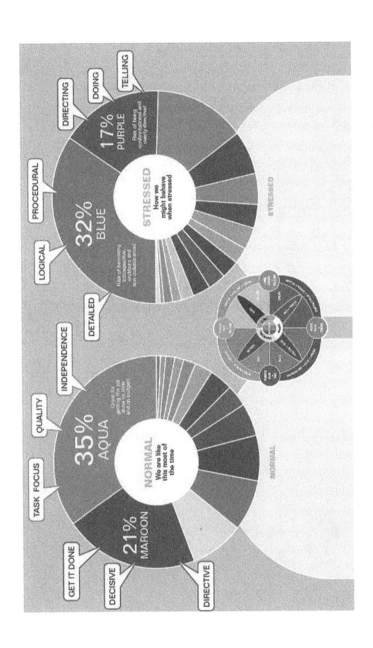

CHAPTER 13

Research Material
and Sources

In this chapter, I wanted to share with you where I got the majority of my information from. I have studied psychology for over 35 years and read hundreds of books on the subject. I have trained in many psychometric models. If you look, you can find that the history, roots, and research for SPECTRUM were mainly from the following work.

I wrote this new model based on the following research, books, and methods by others already widely accepted in their own fields.

1. Psychoanalytical School	Freud	Defense mechanisms
	Adler	Self-motivation not sexual
	Fromm	"Man for Himself"—Behavior types
		Influence of environment and situation
2. Associationists	Locke	The notion of sensory perception
3. Behaviorists	Hume	We pursue knowledge it does not pursue us (nature/nurture debate and free will vs. determinism.
4. Empiricists	Pavlov	Reflex behavior
	Thorndike	Classical and operant conditioning
	Watson	Stimulus response
	Hull	Reinforcement
	Skinner	Shaping
		Positive reinforcement
		Learning theory, selling skills, team dynamics, leadership, token economy, and so on
5. Cognitive element	Broadbent	Problem solving, thinking, memory, combined behavior, and empirical data
	Hebb	Dream theory element

6. Functionalism	Darwin	Animal and herd instinct—grouping and categorizing people
	James	Intelligence and personality tests
7. Gestalt		Patterns of behavior—looking at the whole rather than the component parts
8. Humanistic	Rodgers	Free spirit, generous, potential for growth and learning
		"On becoming a man"
	Maslow	Positive, would/should—self-actualization, maximize one's potential
	Drucker	Questionnaire and case study based, does use experiments and is largely scientific because it has content validity, criterion validity, and construct validity. It looks at style, behavior feelings, and attitude.
9. Personality development	Atkins	33% to 67% rule with 20%
		Dynamic based very loosely on ID, Ego, and Super-Ego.
10. Motivation	Maslow	Hierarchy of needs, needs—basic physiological, advanced, safety, security, love, feelings, belonging, competence, prestige, esteem, self-fulfillment, curiosity, and the need to understand.
11. Physiological and biological	Descartes	Nurture element, reductional element, "Humans have a soul."
12. Howard Gardener's	Seven	Learning intelligences

Title / Author	Extrovert / Task	Extrovert / People	Introvert / People	Introvert / Task
Spectrum / Jarrett	RED	YELLOW	GREEN	BLUE
HIPPOCRATES & GALEN –370BC & 190AD	CHOLERIC	SANGUINE	PHLEGMATIC	MELANCHOLIC
ARISTOTLE -320BC	FIRE/WARM	AIR/COOL	WATER/MOIST	EARTH/DRY
JUNG FUNCTIONS	INTUITION	SENSATION	FEELING	THINKING
FROMM	TAKING	EXCHANGING	ACCEPTING	PRESERVING
KATCHER & ATKINS LIFO	CONTROLLING	ADAPTING	SUPPORTING	CONSERVING
MBTI – Myers-Briggs	EXTROVERT, THINKING, INTUITIVE, PERCEIVING	EXTROVERT, FEELING, SENSING, PERCEIVING	INTROVERT, FEELING, SENSING, JUDGING	INTROVERT, THINKING, INTUITIVE, JUDGING
JUNG – ATTITUDES	PERCEIVING, EXTERNALLY FOCUSED, OBJECTIVE	EXTROVERT, EXTERNALLY FOCUSED, SUBJECTIVE	JUDGING, INTERNALLY FOCUSED SUBJECTIVE	INTROVERT INTERNALLY FOCUSED OBJECTIVE
DISC – THOMAS INTERNATIONAL	DOMININANCE	INFLUENCE	CONSCIENTIOUSNESS	STAEDINESS
SDI	RED	MIX OF ALL THREE	BLUE	GREEN
WATSON & CRICK	ADRENINE	THYAMINE	CYTOSINE	GOANINE
PAVLOV	ENERGETIC	EXCITABLE	INHIBITED	STAEDFAST
IAN TIBBLES ACE	DRIVER	MIXER	HELPER	PLANNER
INSIGHTS	DIRECTOR/REFORMER	INSPIRER/MOTIVATOR	HELPER/SUPPORTER	COORDINATOR/OBSERVER

(Continued)

(Continued)

FACET5	CONTROL/AGGRESSION	ENERGY/HAPPINESS	AFFECTION/SADNESS	WILL/PASSIVITY
PLATO 340BC	INTUITIVE	ARTISTIC	SENSIBLE	REASONED
MAR's Facial Shapes	OVAL	TRIANGULAR	ROUND	SQUARE
KEIRSEY	IDEALIST	ARTISAN	GUARDIAN	RATIONALIST
EMPEDOCLES	FIRE	AIR	EARTH	WATER
HIPPOCRATES	BLOOD	YELLOW BILE	PHLEGM	BLACK BILE
EYSENCK	RESTLESS	LIVELY	CAREFUL	RESERVED
BERZIGER	RESULTS	CREATIVITY	EMPATHY	ROUTINE
BIG 5	EXTROVERT CONFIDENT	EXTROVERT CREATIVE	INTROVERT SENSITIVE	INTROVERT DETAIL
BIRKMAN	AUTHORITY	ACTIVITY	ACCEPTANCE	STRUCTURE
OPQ	EXTROVERT TASK FOCUSED	EXTROVERT PEOPLE FOCUSED	INTROVERT PEOPLE FOCUSED	INTROVERT TASK FOCUSED

CHAPTER 14

Links to Other Sites and Materials

Here are links to some of the other excellent models; please go and try them and then try ours. They are all brilliant, useful, and have a part to play, and you may be wedded to one already. But one big question—why spend hundreds of dollars or pounds on each one when Spectrum does at least 90 percent of what the others do for under £9.99/$14.99. By using the expensive psychometrics and profiling tools ones—it excludes the majority of your fellow work colleagues. Everyone should have access to a simple cheap or free behavioral profile. Most companies spend 90% of their training budget on the top 10 percent of their leadership teams instead of spending 90% on the customer facing staff. Who needs the most help: the successful business leaders or the CUSTOMER FACING STAFF?

Evaluation store—www.evaluationstore.com

MYERS BRIGGS—www.myersbriggs.org/my-mbti-personality-type/mbti-basics/

LIFO—www.lifeorientations.com

DISC—www.ediscprofile.com/?gclid=CLfJ25mO0pgCFZiT3wodak3a0g

ACE—www.pactconsultancy.com/default.asp?page=35

And for personality models, try:

41 QUESTIONS—www.41q.com/

Saville & Holdsworth OPQ—www.shl.com/shl/uk

NEO—http://en.wikipedia.org/wiki/Revised_NEO_Personality_Inventory

Quotes From Readers of the Draft Manuscript

A comprehensive insight into a fascinating topic. With this book, Steve has translated his years of experience, knowledge and expertise into an indispensable guide to behavior. His SPECTRUM model makes a great tool for self-development and working successfully with others. Read and learn.

—MD of Poppyfish People Development Ltd

I have used SPECTRUM many times over the past five years for team exercises, recruitment and individual coaching, and the response and impact has always been positive. This book uncovers the myths and misunderstandings about behavior we have lived with over the years and provides an easy to use guide to behavioral change.

—Julie Sutton, FCIPD

When it comes to developing human performance, awareness of human behavior and its impact on others is a crucial element. This book, through its progressive account of what human behavior actually is and the operating choices we have as humans, gives a practical and systematic model for us all to use—whatever our professional or personal interests are. The key thing is the simplicity but accuracy of the language used. This means everyone can understand and appreciate the Spectrum model so that it can be universally used.

—Dr. Jon Baber

Taking the SPECTRUM profile opened my eyes to a simple behavioral model that was memorable and helpful. This book explains why it works. Read it!

—Nick Skinner, MBA, MSc

There are a vast number of behavioral evaluations available globally in a market worth approx. $4bn. These often seem to overcomplicate their proposition to justify charging $200+ per person. Stephen has gone in the opposite direction and made behavioral evaluation a simple, straight-forward, cost-effective exercise available and affordable to all people. Simply explained and globally available on www.EvaluationStore.com, this should bring professional behavioral evaluation within everybody's budget and save millions of dollars.

—Stephen Berry, author of the books
Strategies of the Serengeti and *Strategy in a Week*

Index

OTHER TITLES IN THE HUMAN RESOURCE MANAGEMENT AND ORGANIZATIONAL BEHAVIOR COLLECTION

- *The New Leader: Harnessing the Power of Creativity to Produce Change* by Renee Kosiarek
- *Performance Leadership* by Karen Moustafa Leonard and Fatma Pakdil
- *Leading the Positive Organization: Actions, Tools, and Processes* by Thomas N. Duening, et al
- *The Illusion of Inclusion: Global Inclusion, Unconscious Bias and the Bottom Line* by Helen Turnbull
- *On All Cylinders: The Entrepreneur's Handbook* by Ron Robinson
- *Employee LEAPS: Leveraging Engagement by Applying Positive Strategies* by Kevin E. Phillips
- *Making Human Resource Technology Decisions: A Strategic Perspective* by Janet H. Marler and Sandra L. Fisher
- *Feet to the Fire: How to Exemplify and Create the Accountability that Creates Great Companies* by Lorraine A. Moore
- *HR Analytics and Innovations in Workforce Planning* by Tony Miller
- *The Real Me: Find and Express Your Authentic Self* by Mark Eyre

Announcing the Business Expert Press Digital Library

Concise e-books business students need for classroom and research

This book can also be purchased in an e-book collection by your library as

- a one-time purchase,
- that is owned forever,
- allows for simultaneous readers,
- has no restrictions on printing, and
- can be downloaded as PDFs from within the library community.

Our digital library collections are a great solution to beat the rising cost of textbooks. E-books can be loaded into their course management systems or onto students' e-book readers.
The **Business Expert Press** digital libraries are very affordable, with no obligation to buy in future years. For more information, please visit **www.businessexpertpress.com/librarians**. To set up a trial in the United States, please email **sales@businessexpertpress.com**.

CPSIA information can be obtained
at www.ICGtesting.com
Printed in the USA
FSHW021654080220
66791FS